THROUGH
THEIR EYES

FUTURE ECHOES
Edited By Jess Giaffreda

First published in Great Britain in 2020 by:

Young Writers
Remus House
Coltsfoot Drive
Peterborough
PE2 9BF
Telephone: 01733 890066
Website: www.youngwriters.co.uk

All Rights Reserved
Book Design by Ashley Janson
© Copyright Contributors 2019
Softback ISBN 978-1-83928-772-5

Printed and bound in the UK by BookPrintingUK
Website: www.bookprintinguk.com
YB0432W

FOREWORD

Since 1991, here at Young Writers we have celebrated the awesome power of creative writing, especially in young adults, where it can serve as a vital method of expressing strong (and sometimes difficult) emotions, a conduit to develop empathy, and a safe, non-judgemental place to explore one's own place in the world. With every poem we see the effort and thought that each pupil published in this book has put into their work and by creating this anthology we hope to encourage them further with the ultimate goal of sparking a life-long love of writing.

Through Their Eyes challenged young writers to open their minds and pen bold, powerful poems from the points-of-view of any person or concept they could imagine – from celebrities and politicians to animals and inanimate objects, or even just to give us a glimpse of the world as they experience it. The result is this fierce collection of poetry that by turns questions injustice, imagines the innermost thoughts of influential figures or simply has fun.

The nature of the topic means that contentious or controversial figures may have been chosen as the narrators, and as such some poems may contain views or thoughts that, although may represent those of the person being written about, by no means reflect the opinions or feelings of either the author or us here at Young Writers.

We encourage young writers to express themselves and address subjects that matter to them, which sometimes means writing about sensitive or difficult topics. If you have been affected by any issues raised in this book, details on where to find help can be found at *www.youngwriters.co.uk/info/other/contact-lines*

CONTENTS

Abbot Beyne School, Burton-On-Trent

Katie Owen (14)   1

Campsmount Academy, Norton

Kaci Porritt (14)   2

Crestwood Community School, Eastleigh

Rovens Nolbergs (13)   3
Shana Smith (12)   4
Jay Alexander Hawkins (13)   5
Lucy Dancy (12)   6
Freya Evans (12)   7
Kyle Dobie (12)   8
Erin Chandler (13)   9
Summer Doherty (12)   10

Fulston Manor School, Sittingbourne

Aimee Rebecca Moultrie (14)   11
Spike Sweeney (15)   12
Thomas Goldsmith (12)   15
Luke Blades (11)   16
Reva Ahluwalia (11)   17
Kimberly Alexis Singer (18)   18
Jack Thomas (11)   19

Harrogate Ladies' College, Harrogate

Zoe Man (18)   20
Emily-Anne Jones   23
Matilda Page (13)   24

Amelie Coyle (12)   26
Eve Brasher (14)   29
Kayla Smith (15)   30
Milly Taylor (16)   32
Alexa Brooke Monts De Oca (12)   34
Helia Mirakhori (14)   36
Phoebe Russell (14)   38
Caitlin Stott (13)   39
Ruth Caroline Kendrick (14)   40
Chloe van Vliet (12)   41
Lucinda Weston (13)   42

Lutterworth High School, Lutterworth

William Dewes (12)   43
Romany Williams (12)   44
Charlotte Ward (11)   45

Mallaig High School, Mallaig

Lee McLean   46
Laila Tarn   47
Ellie MacKay   48
Finn Geddes   49

Millside School - Haybrook College, Slough

Chelsea Butler   50
Mikey Hoad   51
Harry Hewett   52
Taylor Stevens   53

President Kennedy School, Holbrooks

Hana Rashid (12)	54
Maab Hejaaji (11)	58
Tayla-Louise Wing (12)	61
Milo Shakespeare (11)	62
Lara Krefta (12)	64
Shanuja Elangeswaran (11)	66
Ellis James Harridence (11)	68
Abbie Clarke (11)	69
Ethan Moore (11)	70
Isabelle May Betts (12)	71
Shiv Nagra (11)	72
Kristina Popovic (11)	73
Ameera Bawazir (11)	74
Cailey Rushton (11)	75
Inaya Ratiq (11)	76
Diwan Kadr (11)	77

Priory School, Southsea

Seren Jones	78
Marianne Grace McIntyre (11)	80

Queen Elizabeth's Grammar School, Blackburn

Jasmine Georgy (11)	82

Richard Taunton Sixth Form College, Southampton

Victoria Wreford (16)	84
Rhiannon Natalya Kimber (16)	86
Ben Jefferis (17)	87

Somervale School, Midsomer Norton

Trevane Dante Winditt (13)	88
Aoife Duggan-Lee	90
Katie Marie Smith (13)	91
Ryan Hitchens (11)	92
Izabella Gardiner	93

St Aidan's CE Academy, Darlington

Alfie Taylor (11)	94
Lily Potter (11)	95
Mollie Pinkney (11)	96

St John Rigby College, Orrell

Abigail Eve Donlon (17)	97
Holly Fairhurst (16)	98
Heather Ann Tully-Bolton (16)	100
Oskar Leonard (16)	101
Caner Aydin (16)	102

St John's Catholic Comprehensive School, Gravesend

Milvydas Sadauskas (12)	103
Brodie Lynch (11)	104
Jeena Bhanot (12)	105

Villiers High School, Southall

Anjali Banger (12)	106
Ayuub Siad (14)	109
Sanika Kiritharan (12)	110
Mathusha Vijayarasa (12)	112
Jaskaran Singh Lamba (11)	114
Prisha Prisha (11)	116
Maegan Fernandes (13)	118
Georgina Shinoj (13)	120
Denisa Chaves (11)	122
Sumaya Abdirahman (12)	124
Rayan Bhuiyan	126
Rayhan Pathak (12)	128
Maaria Mohamed (14)	130
Sukhraj Singh Nagra (13)	132
Jasmine Robinson (13)	134
Diya Jhamat (13)	136
Maleia Dayo Olateju (13)	138
Nithush Gunarajah (13)	139
Haaniah Zymal Cadar (11)	140
Mathumigaa Kugatheesan (13)	141
Mischa Fernandes (11)	142
Japji Kaur Sahota (11)	143

Rishiban Rahuban (11)	144
Zainab Shah (12)	146
Swechha Dahal (11)	148
Kamaldeep Rehal (13)	150
Yaqub Bodak Jaan (12)	151
Epziba Paramasivam (12)	152
Cavan Goes (13)	153
Kirath Pal (12)	154
Sukhmani Bhachu (11)	156
Hatim (12)	157
Munazza Khalid (13)	158
Himesh Vijai Valgi (12)	159
Yash Sangani (13)	160
Deepshika Kamalakasan (11)	161
Mian Waleed Ahmad (13)	162
Kahin Alemayehu (11)	164
Aditya Bhandari (12)	166
Abdirahman Awmusse (11)	167
Zakaria Abdelrahman (12)	168
Priyesh Kanji (13)	169
Kamaljeet Kukrija (12)	170
Yuvika Tulcidas (12)	172
Muhammed Hassan Abdulmanem (11)	173
Harshpreet Kaur (11)	174
Ridwanul Yamim (12)	175
Anoshan Selvanathan (14)	176
Navdeep Kaur (11)	177
Mustafa Suleman (13)	178
Safa Noor Aurangzaib (13)	179
Agreem Pradhan (13)	180
Iqbal Garewal (11)	181
Ines Ranzan Shil (12)	182
Johan Virgil Mariyathas (12)	184
Hibo Omar Abdallah (11)	185
Musabeha Tuqeer Cheema (14)	186
Ashwinder Kaur (12)	187
Amadou Bente Diallo (12)	188
Jagman Singh (11)	189
Shreya Jadeja (11)	190
Oshita Katial (12)	191
Najma Muhyidin Bundid (11)	192
Arashnoor Singh (11)	193
Jayden Masih (11)	194
Jamal Aidan Khan (11)	195
Maham Fatima Ashraf Begum (11)	196
Bedanta Mukhopadhay (12)	197
Nadal Makoto Spencer-Jennings (12)	198
Manal Khan (12)	199
Diya Patel (12)	200
Arthy Vasikaran (11)	201
Piranusha Mohanathas (12)	202
Kelsi Ramsey-Carney (11)	203
Jaslin Malotra (13)	204
Ramisa Ali (13)	205
Kaelem Rai (13)	206
Anson Fernandes (11)	207
Julinka Pereira (12)	208
Abdul Asslan (12)	209
Inaya Ahmed (11)	210
Tarnbeer Singh (13)	211
Murthad Abdalla (11)	212

Ysgol Brynrefail, Caernarfon

Beca Fon Parry (13)	213

Ysgol Clywedog, Wrexham

Libby Cole (13)	215
Atiya Ahmed (12)	216
Sarah Roberts (13)	217

THE
POEMS

Writer

Ink against the line,
trying to make my words combine.
Letters controlling my imagination,
without any hesitation.

Page after page,
not working, no change.
Books in stores,
for everyone to adore.

A character is named Sodapop,
he never sits at a desktop.
He is always full of charm,
and is also very calm.

Children under fifteen,
have the same favourite scene.
I have had an impact on many lives,
a new journey finally arrives.

Katie Owen (14)
Abbot Beyne School, Burton-On-Trent

Why?

I'm sat in front of my mirror
Wondering, *why me?*
Why?
What did I ever do to them?

I'm here, lying in my bed
The sound of my alarm makes me sick.
I beg and beg to stay at home
Because all I want is to be alone.

I just wish they'd leave me be
And let me be
I'm forever hurting
Why's it always me?

Kaci Porritt (14)
Campsmount Academy, Norton

Winter's Revenge

On a cold night, winter had enough of its rivals,
The wind engulfing everything with its frozen teeth,
Winter was finally in power, because of its arrival,
It was ready to become a thief.

Winter had a plan to attack, any moment,
However, the other seasons had to stop it,
Suddenly, an arctic blow was released as payment,
The other seasons tried but couldn't block it.

They kept fighting with all their might,
But it was no match for winter's power,
Eventually, it all ended and there was no light,
It was the end, there was no answer.

The barren land was coated in a white blanket,
Winter won,
And now everyone had to wear a jacket.

Rovens Nolbergs (13)
Crestwood Community School, Eastleigh

Lone Wolf

I didn't want any of this,
I just wanted to be noticed.
I wanted to eat the meat, not the bone.
I wanted to sleep in the warmth.
I wanted a place to call home.

I didn't mean to cause a riot,
I didn't want a fight.
I didn't want to bleed out
into the winter night.

When we went hunting,
I didn't want to hunt the deer.
They had such fun lives,
but when they saw us, it was all fear.

When I finally left, they called after me,
asking me to stay,
telling me not to flee.
I never understood what happened that night.

But
I am a lone wolf
and that is who I'm supposed to be.

Shana Smith (12)
Crestwood Community School, Eastleigh

I'm Done With This War

The GIs and Tommys
They call us 'Huns'
The pride of our countries
Pushing us on
The Messerschmitt and Mustangs
Their engines hum
I'm done with this war, done and done.

A searing pain in my leg
Am I shot? Am I dead?
Blood still pours
They wrap me up and I'm out cold
I'm done with this war, done and done.

Where am I?
What have they done?
What have we done?
My country's not powerful
I feel no pride
Ashamed, bewildered
Who have I become?
I'm done with this war, done and done.

Jay Alexander Hawkins (13)
Crestwood Community School, Eastleigh

Mental Health

People suffer from poor mental health every day,
Yet we do nothing.
When people ask if you're okay,
You don't say a thing.

If you think your friend is suffering,
Don't tell a teacher,
Just be there if they need comforting,
But telling people can make them feel weaker.

Poor mental health is rising,
And suicidal rates are getting higher.
The percentage of self-harm is climbing,
And look out, because bullying has gone cyber.

Lucy Dancy (12)
Crestwood Community School, Eastleigh

Fishing

I'd rather be fishing,
Most of the time, morning or night,
Rain or shine.

I'll catch 'em,
I'll weigh 'em,
And put 'em all back.
Once we start catching,
We won't ever stop!

Just set up the bivvies,
Show me the rods,
When we go fishing, we won't stop.

I'd rather be fishing,
Most of the time, morning or night,
Rain or shine.

Freya Evans
Crestwood Community School, Eastleigh

Don't Blink

In the room, again,
Twilight shining,
Yet you look,
Why?

When you blink,
I become free,
Free to explore,
To *crunch!*

You fall,
Neck snapped,
Sadness,
Yet I'm free.

My stony legs scrape,
As a scream is heard,
My next destination, perhaps?

No, just a siren,
Yet I am free.

So, blink,
Or don't?

Kyle Dobie (12)
Crestwood Community School, Eastleigh

Donald Trump

Donald Trump who smells like trumps,
Fires missiles all day.
Nobody likes him except for his lovers,
But soon they all go away.

I know people have their own opinions that they want to say,
I know that people support him and that's for them to say.
But for the rest of us, we want him sent away,
No hard feelings, for this is our way.

Erin Chandler (13)
Crestwood Community School, Eastleigh

Sandwiches

I am a sandwich,
I am very tasty,
I look like a yummy piece of bread
With golden butter,
With cheese and ham,
With bloody-looking tomato,
Brown, crispy bacon
You can have me warm or cold,
Either way, I am very tasty.
Sandwiches are easy to make for picnics
And they're good for lunchboxes.

Summer Doherty (12)
Crestwood Community School, Eastleigh

Lost And Found

I've been sitting on this shelf for decades on end
And all the other books are always on lend
I'm dusty and dirty
And I've never been opened
I'm lonely and grumpy
And I'll remain unspoken.

One day, touched by a hand
Someone reads me as planned
I'm free at last and ready to explore
"Take me home with you to read!" I implore.

"Oh no!" I shout
I'm soaked to the core
There's coffee all over me
I'm thrown to the floor!
I need to go, I need to flee
Before anyone else tries to ruin me.

I'm ripped and torn like a stag losing his horn
Thrown and discarded
Constantly being bombarded
I cry, I weep
I need to sleep
Put me back on the shelf
So I can be by myself...

Aimee Rebecca Moultrie (14)
Fulston Manor School, Sittingbourne

The Farmer

The sun beats down,
cracking down like a burning whip,
scorching the already desolate plains dry,
yet, nought was as dry as my face.

My eyes are swollen and burnt,
like two empty swimming pools,
boiling the shrivelled sockets,
to withered blood sacks.

To the left, where the livestock once stood,
saviours in the sun,
ox, a sheep, a cow,
only brittle and crumbling bones linger now,
part of the pen toppled over where the wise ones choose to flee and fly,
to greener, cooler lands.

The plants would flee if they could,
uproot themselves from the cursed soil and infertile wastes and run,
yet, nonetheless,
they're bound to me to the death,
which will come soon.

Refugees, migrants and the 'real victims' of the world live better than I,
in the desert, all alone,

in a slumdog, ramshackle hut,
the walls, twisted steel that burns fierce in the sun,
so much so that, if I or any other man should simply caress it,
their hands would burn, brand, fester and peel like a serpent's hide,
throbbing in agonising repetition and pain.

I often go to sleep at night with my ribs and chest bursting through my tight skin,
my fingers are like thin fingers with razor, unkempt nails at the end,
my belly a cold, vacant ditch that's never full,
my heart a pale, thumping fistful of red meat,
that drones incessantly through night and day.

When you look to the sky with its vast expanses and perpetual scenery,
you don't see a white cloud or a grey rain cloud,
no, you only see the wretched red sunset shaded with a vain orange,
with the same relentless blue sky rolling on.

You see, I, the farmer, am a very bitter fellow,
I scold the blue sky whilst you praise it,
I damn the orange sun whilst you admire it,
I rue the vain red sunset whilst you love it,
you have eyes to see, yet you don't use them to look my way,
you have ears to hear the news of our suffering, yet you've heard it all before,

you don't have time for the farmers' lives,
so I'll disappear like the rest,
right underneath the burning sun.

Spike Sweeney (15)
Fulston Manor School, Sittingbourne

Heroes

Heroes
Who are they?
Can they fly like Superman
Or wear shining armour?

Can they defeat villains
And use a Lightsaber?
Or run fast as light
Be skilled with a bow and arrow?

Maybe I see them every day
Out in the streets
With no powers
Just trying to make a change.

The military defending our country
Nelson Mandela standing up for what is right
The police protecting the innocent
Or are we the people who will make the change?

We could be those heroes
Fight for what we believe
Protecting the ones we love
That's heroic, you are too.

I am one of those heroes
Just like you
You don't know who I am or who I'll be
But together, we can make history.

Thomas Goldsmith (12)
Fulston Manor School, Sittingbourne

The Life Of A Cup!

As I'm pulled out of the dark, gloomy cupboard, I sense excitement, as the light overwhelms me.
Suddenly, I see liquid poured into me as I slowly drown.
Help!
This isn't what I wanted!
Suddenly, I loved the cupboard. It was the best place in the world!
Please put me back!
I don't like this!
Burble burble
Help! Please!
Arghhh...
It's over.
Finally.
I don't like it here.
I try to roll over.
I can't.
Oh no!
A human
I try to escape, but I can't. It's walking towards me.
It picks me up. Aaargh! Not again!
Oh. It's over. Home sweet home.
Aaargh! Again?

Luke Blades (11)
Fulston Manor School, Sittingbourne

Life Of A Dog

I love smelling new things,
I love meeting new things.

I want to know how my owner sees me,
I hope it's different to how I see myself.

To be a good pet, I have to be a loyal carer,
A guard.

At times, I get confused,
Which gives me the blues.

I look up at her, my eyes gleaming,
Hoping that she won't tell me off.

Reva Ahluwalia (11)
Fulston Manor School, Sittingbourne

Lost In The Ebony Flow Of Time

A thousand doors and a mountain so high
I'm trapped
The future is cruel
It forces us to look upon our demons
And scream!
I'm drowning
Iron bars stay firmly locked
An army rises upon the barren land
Yet, there's no one who stands beside me
I wish I was lost in the ebony flow of time
Where actions bear no consequence.

Kimberly Alexis Singer (18)
Fulston Manor School, Sittingbourne

Game

I'm alive,
I just pop,
Out of thin air.
I move,
But no,
I don't want to,
But I move,
Off,
Off a cliff,
I fall,
Oof!
I hit the ground,
I can't move.

I come back,
I can move,
But not the way I want,
Off again.

Jack Thomas (11)
Fulston Manor School, Sittingbourne

Seasons Of Love

My world was a blank slate, a fresh start;
A spring full of possibilities.
Her mahogany eyes met mine,
And crisp green grass breaks through
The surface of my icy heart.
A surge of warmth pumps through my veins.
Her hand brushes against mine,
A trail of daisies blooms from the ground
Where her porcelain skin had caressed.
My senses abruptly shock back to life,
Cultivating hope, passion and joy,
Masking the dead carcasses of
Pain, hatred and disdain
That were buried under the soulless permafrost.

Her soft lips graze against mine,
Blood rushes to my cheeks
As summer kisses them crimson.
Torrential downpours of hate
Can hail down on us,
But we take it in our stride.
We throw our umbrellas aside
And drench ourselves to the core.
The world may try to freeze our love stagnant,
But with every touch, every kiss,
The fire rekindles
And our hearts beat on.

The heat starts to fade into
The decaying chill of autumn.
The bed grows cold as
An eerie breeze wafts through the grey curtains.
A single leaf brushes past us as
The wind howls in the background,
Screaming, begging for a conversation.
We stare into each other's eyes,
Now as empty and hollow as
The miserable mahogany tree whose
Few hopeful remaining leaves
Cling onto what is left of us.

Then comes the blizzard,
The wintry monster bred from
Ignorance and abandonment.
The wind howls louder and louder
And eventually,
In comes the torrent of hail and frost,
Our visions impaired by
The needles of icicles hurtling towards us,
The truth masked by
Flurries of snow.
With rational thoughts frozen
In the depths of our heads,
Bladed words hurl towards each other
With no regard for consequence.

I look away,
Tear streaks frozen into my cheekbones.
The wind starts to die,
Reason thaws my rigid mind.
Just as I turn around to break the ice,
The gale has already ripped her away from me.
I collapse onto the thick blanket of snow,
Cries of pain, hatred and disdain
Break through the cracks of the permafrost
And its pathetic echoes seep into mankind.
Icy walls rise around me,
Protecting, insulating me,
But in an effort to shield me from pain,
It freezes my heart
And the belief that I could ever love anyone
Ever again.

That is
Until his hazel eyes meet mine.
Although my heart is frozen solid,
With a little extra warmth,
It softens,
And the seasons of love start all over again.

Zoe Man (18)
Harrogate Ladies' College, Harrogate

Hidden War

People are dying, there's no use in dreaming
It happens so often you can't hear them screaming
But what can we do? When will we see
That there's more to this than just you or me?

Children with no wish of fighting
Running away from bombs like lightning.
They're stuck out there, that's their home
Starving hungry, just skin and bone.

They have no choice but to stay
Wherever they go, they can't get away.
They're trapped over there, trapped in their skin
Trapped in their heads, they'll just never win.

They're fighting a war of a different sort
Whilst you're over here at a fancy resort
Fancy clothes and fancy shoes
Fancy drinks and fancy food.

No one has that, it's not fair
People are stuck, crying and scared
Stuck 'cause of money, 'cause of war, 'cause of famine
Stuck with decisions they don't get a choice in.

People are dying, there's no use in dreaming
It happens so often you can't hear them screaming
But what can we do? When will we see
That there's more to this world than just you or me?

Emily-Anne Jones
Harrogate Ladies' College, Harrogate

The War Which Tore Us All

On this day, my daddy went to war,
and this is the day our family tore.
The streets were empty and scarily cold,
but the rest of the day was yet to unfold.
The walls were shaking and the sky was dark grey,
but why oh why did our family have to pay?

Up the stairs and round the corner,
lay a full straw sack full of supplies and water.
Daddy was a big worrier, you see,
always twitching if he was late for tea.
But now Daddy will never be here for supper,
he'll be either down a steep trench or maybe later in a gutter.

Then I heard heavy footsteps plodding down the stairs,
big heavy boots were making the thin carpet tear.
Daddy was wearing his neatest clothes,
but despite his effort, you could still see his cheeky big toes!
I looked up at Daddy and gave him a grin,
but whilst I was smiling, I felt the tears roll down my chin.

I clenched my teddy with all my might,
whilst I gave Daddy a hug which was ever so tight.
His prickly felt blazer was rubbing harshly against my cheek,
and eventually, by now, I was starting to weep.
Daddy's kind hands were like crashing waves,
rolling gently down my back in huge cascades.

My salty tears had made my face all inflamed and red.
"Stay strong, my little tiger." At least, that's what I recall he said.
His tight grip was starting to fade,
but I couldn't just let him fade away.
What, oh what were we going to do?
Without Daddy, we were doomed.

He tossed his straw sack over his shoulder,
it looked so heavy, it was like a giant boulder.
Daddy was strongly holding back the tears,
I bet he was thinking about all of his fears.
Mummy and Daddy gave each other a kiss,
whilst Daddy was staring into the great abyss.

Daddy opened the door, which came flinging open,
and the gust of cold, crisp air made us all feel broken.
The frozen tears in my eyes were like an ocean,
what would I do with all this commotion?
He stared at us all for one last time,
Mummy, my brother, the dog and I.

He said one last thing before he left,
one last thing before he left the nest.
With his tears in his eyes and his maroon cap up in his hand,
he whispered one thing, one thing which he had planned.
"If I die, my children, do not cry,
but just look up at the sky and say goodbye."

Matilda Page (13)
Harrogate Ladies' College, Harrogate

The Velvety Bunny

I am The Velvety Bunny, I'm cute and never complain
I'd never want to hurt a human
Or cause them any pain
My midnight fur is soft as clouds, my eyes glitter like stars
I'm warm like a hot water bottle
And cuddly like a scarf
One day, I was taken
From my home and family
I was taken by a human
And her name was Jinny Lee
She put me in a cage
It was dark and cold and damp
There was an icy breeze from the window sill
And there wasn't even a lamp
Then one day, someone lets me out
My luck is getting brighter
They lift me onto a table
Where I see on it a lighter
But then, suddenly, I'm pinned right down, my head slams on the table
My lip starts trembling
And I feel really unstable
The man takes out a little pot and towards me he glides
Leaning right over my face
And out his hand slides
Then suddenly, it's agony, I try and squirm about

For my eye feels like it's burning
And is going to ooze right out
I'd rather die than go through this, the most excruciating, utter anguish
I cannot see, I squirm and squeal
I'm screaming for my family
I'm screaming for this torture to end
I'm screaming for someone to come and help
But all the man does is watch and note
Watch and note, watch and note
He does not care about my pain
He does not care about my eye
He does not care that it's burning
Burning, burning
Right out.

That was the first time this new life started
A life of pain and torture
Sometimes, it's even worse than that
I can't take it any longer
My eyes don't glitter anymore, I cannot even see
My midnight fur is scabby and bloody
So I can no longer be
The Velvety Bunny
That's not my name
For my fur has lost its velvet
Now, I am The Blind Bunny
The Blind Bunny, The Blind Bunny

I am The Blind Bunny
I'm not cute and have no way to complain
I thought hurting a human would be rather mean
I never thought they'd be the ones to cause me pain.

Amelie Coyle (12)
Harrogate Ladies' College, Harrogate

Gone In A Blink

Whether they chirp, meow or bark
Or whether you take them to the park
Pets are always there by your side
Waiting to be loved, waiting to be identified.

But yet, our lives are so busy with school, technology and stress
We ignore them and focus on the latest trend or mess
They smother us with love if we give them the slightest bit of attention
Though it does not last long, should I mention.

Before you know it, they start to fade away
And that's when I try to say
"Make the most of your pet being alive!"
Yet, you ignore me and, without them, continue to thrive.

What seems like a millisecond later, they are gone
All that's left is silence and scorn
For you ask yourself, full of regret
"Why did I never play with my pet?"

Because, my friend, you never thought of them and time
And this is where I end my rhyme.

Eve Brasher (14)
Harrogate Ladies' College, Harrogate

#loveyourself

It was easier to love someone else
Than it was to love myself.
The standards I had set
Ate at me
Hurt me
And tore me apart
'Til I met her
The calico cat, my euphoria
And at that point, I had a epiphany
I thought that this might be my fortunate stroke of serendipity
To show me
The truth untold
Telling me to stop this fake love
And to be thankful for what I had and what I was
To be thankful for my DNA.

Blood, sweat and tears
I had shed them all throughout my life...
Until now
Until I discovered the best of me
From now on, I will be my own idol.

So what?
So what if they call me right or wrong?
I won't remain on this broken seesaw that has kept me down all those years

I can finally say, "I'm fine."
I can just dance without a care
I can fall in love
And I have finally realised I am a singularity in this world and...
I am unique.

And with that realisation, I shed a tear among the many from the past
But this one is different from the rest
It is a tear of pure happiness
Not a tear of pain, sorrow or despair
From this day on, I start my new journey
From here, I depart on the first part of my journey and leave behind my fear
And climb aboard Airplane Pt 2
My new beginning.

Over time, I wander aimlessly, 'til I step inside my magic shop
The place I will find my missing self
And become my own Anpanman
The heroine of my own story.

And now my story has come to an end
As I watch the mic drop
I have found my answer.

I have learnt to love myself.

Kayla Smith (15)
Harrogate Ladies' College, Harrogate

So Easily Lost

They didn't know what they were doing,
Neither you or I can blame them for the destruction of a weak mind.
My heart was only a flower among the bushes of their boyish playing.
You tread without notice, you took without seeing, so now you mustn't be blind.

Now they know, now they see the deep scarlet evil within,
They shriek songs of sorrow and shatter the delicate glass of sanity.
The house is barren; it's all gone, every frame, every memory of what could have been.
All they do is sit in a silent room with nothing but an abyss of vanity.

They order drink after drink, acting like starved animals in the frosty winter.
His cold and careless heart is being filled with hatred for this eternal freeze and me.
But that changes.
When days like spring come, the room glows gold and I think he can see my face.

Now he greets it with a smile,
A knowing look I know too well.
The smile I gave him once in a while...

Off I went after the shouting, after the ignorance and after the bell.

I swapped places with my murderer and soon, very soon, we will speak again.

Milly Taylor (16)
Harrogate Ladies' College, Harrogate

Save Our Future

Can you hear the trees crashing,
the ice melting,
hear the mournful whale song,
the animals running for their lives,
the voices protesting?

Can you see the white rhinos,
orangutans, the tigers, vanishing,
the islands of plastic floating,
the open plains once shrouded with trees,
the sea rising like one big bathtub?

Can you feel the heat consuming us,
the water warming,
the air changing,
the pressure to help stop this,
the planet becoming unsustainable?

Can you smell the diesel fumes,
the toxic air,
the burning fossil fuels,
the bitter ash of forest fumes,
the heavy, looming smog from the cities?

Can you sense the desperation,
from everyone, everywhere?
Will you save our future while you can?

All of this, but for what, money?
Help! Help! Help!

Alexa Brooke Monts De Oca (12)
Harrogate Ladies' College, Harrogate

The Unseen One

I am a king.
I stay passive amongst the shadows,
where I am the god of the dead.
The humans cower down to me,
too afraid to even whisper my name:
Hades.

One brother rules the skies,
another the sea.
The people give them temples, sanctuaries,
when I,
I am given nothing.

Alone.
I drew the short straw,
left to be the caretaker of the souls.
Talk about unlucky.

An eternity passed
in darkness,
until
I met her.

Persephone was majestic,
Aphrodite would pale in comparison.
Soon enough, I realised,
there was no other option.
She had to be mine,

and so,
I took her.

The pomegranate.
Six sanguine seeds
sealed her fate
as my queen.

I was no longer alone.

Helia Mirakhori (14)
Harrogate Ladies' College, Harrogate

Death, Social Media And Death

Social media and death,
What's the link?
Death, suicide, murder,
Dying.

Life on this Earth was made to be lived,
But social media didn't agree with that,
Snapchat didn't agree with that,
But death did.

Life was made to be fun,
But Instagram didn't agree with that,
Perfect people, perfect bodies, perfect lives,
I knew it wasn't my time to be alive.

I saw the knife,
My beautiful life was ending,
I picked it up,
I knew my life was pending.

Faster and faster,
My silence grew louder,
And all I knew was:
Although the silence may carry on,
I knew that soon I would be gone.

Phoebe Russell (14)
Harrogate Ladies' College, Harrogate

The End Is... Tonight

Twenty-five or twenty-eight,
How many days until my fate?
Now I have reached the lowest of low,
This is the dreaded death row.

Sitting at my cell's table,
A guard comes and hands me a label.
Lifting it into the window light,
My life is scheduled to end tonight.

I'm thrown into an unknown room,
Squinting my eyes, they adjust to the gloom,
There sits the furniture I hoped I wouldn't see,
Now it will steal my life from me.

A hand shoves me towards the chair,
Deeper and deeper into the lair,
The switch is flicked and the current grows,
This is the dreaded death row...

Caitlin Stott (13)
Harrogate Ladies' College, Harrogate

Watching After

I float up in the kitchen and watch as you stumble past,
Collecting all the cards and binning them fast.
You can hear them all droning, "Sorry for your loss,"
Whilst you think about the headstone that will soon be covered in moss.

The rope around my neck holds me above the ground,
You have to understand that my choices were bound.
The letter that I left flutters to the ground,
I had to leave this godforsaken ground.

You fall to the ground, letting out a strangled cry,
Your tears drip from your eyes that are never dry.
I am sorry that I left you,
But you should have known why.

Ruth Caroline Kendrick (14)
Harrogate Ladies' College, Harrogate

Death Row

I sit on my rusted bed and sigh
Wiping tears yet to dry
Because each day, it could be my turn to die.

Thirty-one states
Where I would remain an inmate
But nobody outruns fate.

What words do you want to be remembered by?
What word do you you want to scream or utter?
More importantly, how do I control my stutter?

For this is worse than performing live
You have one chance to truly surprise
To shed your lies and guise.

Worse yet, you don't know
How you will finally go
But such is life on death row.

Chloe van Vliet (12)
Harrogate Ladies' College, Harrogate

Prisoner Of War

Trapped,
Trapped in my own body,
Trapped in the four walls,
Trapped behind the barbed wires.

Help,
Help me escape,
Help me live,
Help me conquer the darkness.

Escape,
I need to escape,
Escape from this life,
This is not a life.

Death,
Death is my friend,
Death is my family,
Death in me.

Lucinda Weston (13)
Harrogate Ladies' College, Harrogate

A Mirror's View

I'm reflective and adjustable,
seeing cars every day,
crawling along the fields, watching all the work.
Ploughing, sowing, baling, flicking up the dirt.
Spring, summer, autumn, moving all day long.
In the winter, I'm a stationary soul,
tucked up in my shed,
all dusty and cold.

In the spring, I'm awakened,
brought back to life,
feeding the cows and turning the soil,
spraying the crops,
the engine a-toil.

In the summer, I'll see the combine,
loading up my trailer,
with a waterfall of golden corn,
setting my vision ablaze.

As autumn ripens, I start sowing once more,
life is born again for the ancient ground,
with seeds of birth being planted.

Finally, back in winter, tucked alone in my shed,
darkness and dust obscure my views,
as the world outside continues.

William Dewes (12)
Lutterworth High School, Lutterworth

What Is A Book?

A book is a dream you can hold
A book is a story untold
A book will be your best friend
A book will never end.

What is a book?

Books can be scary or funny
Books can put butterflies in your tummy
Books are many shapes and sizes
Books are your very own prizes.

What is a book?

A book can be about villains or heroes
A book can be full of numbers or zeroes
A book can bring tears of joy
A book can be about a girl or boy.

What is a book?

A book can be anything!

Romany Williams (12)
Lutterworth High School, Lutterworth

Untitled

The bear
Strong, aggressive
But sweet and kind
They have dark brown fur
And hazelnut eyes.

The dog
Protective and sweet
Cute and furry
Small or big
Brown or white
They're a dog
And that's what I like.

The eagle
Soaring across the sky
Looking bold and brave
Observing for their prey
Which they see at day.

Charlotte Ward (11)
Lutterworth High School, Lutterworth

Fishing

T here're seagulls chasing a fishing boat.
H ow do the fishermen cope with the seagulls all the time? They must be annoying.
R aging fishermen gutting their fish on the boat.
O pening the barrel then putting the scraps in it.
U p in the wheelhouse, driving the boat into the harbour.
G etting ready to arrive in the harbour.
H auling our creels with excitement.

T here are four velvet crabs in the creel.
H igh tide with my fishing rod.
E ager to catch some fish - preferably mackerel.
I 'm delighted, I got a huge mackerel.
R unning down to my friends to show them how big it was.

E ventually, after ten minutes or so, I get another one, but this time it is just a cuddie.
Y earling, the fish is.
E ventually, it is time to go home.
S eeing the seagulls as I go home.

Lee McLean
Mallaig High School, Mallaig

Through The Barbed Wire

Stripes, stripes of guards, stripes of light, stripes of nothing
No longer wanted, no longer needed, not allowed to school
People on the street like to shout and scream at me
And hide their eyes as not to see.

This world is not for me, but for them, but they will see
They will see, I will be free
But it's hard to be free when you are segregated from society
My friends have turned on me because of their families
And there are no more places for me
But then I had hoped to go to where they said it would be good, fun, exciting and new
But they were wrong.

I was on a train for what seemed to be too long
But then all fell silent, you could hear a pin drop
Then the bitter wind hit my face and I saw stripes of light in my face and the moon shining like there was no tomorrow
But for many, there wasn't.

Laila Tarn
Mallaig High School, Mallaig

Dogs Love Their Owners!

D ancing and prancing around, just waiting for her!
O h, I will be so happy when she comes.
G alloping around, oh, where is she?
S tanding there for another hour.

L ater and later, the day goes on.
O kay, now I am on the couch,
V ery tired.
E ventually, I fall asleep.

T wo hours later.
H appily arisen from my sleep.
E verything is blurry.
I hear noises getting louder and louder!
R acing to the door!

O pening the door, here she is!
W hining madly, I jump on her.
N ext, another hour goes by.
E ventually, I get my dinner.
R eally, I love my owner.

Ellie MacKay
Mallaig High School, Mallaig

The New Kid

T hrough their eyes, I look at the new kid
H ollow they are
R espectful, no doubt
O bliging he is
U nselfish he looks
G enerous, all so kind
H eart-warming he can be.

T alented he truly is
H elpful he is
E ffort he has for everything he does
I ntelligent in everything
R esponsible he always is.

E ntertaining to watch, a laugh he is
Y oung and thoughtful, all so true
E nergetic, all so quick
S uccessful, what a kid.

Finn Geddes
Mallaig High School, Mallaig

The Good Gang

The thought of being in a gang makes me feel sad
Those lovely young people trying to act bad
Joining a gang, they think they'll be okay
Until the time that they don't see another day.

Lack of understanding of the risks that await
Some people just get led trying to find a soulmate
Young people, it's so dangerous out there
Life is so precious and some people really don't care.

Follow your role models, be the best you can be
So many opportunities and so many great things to see
Work hard, play hard and do your very best
Stay true to yourself and don't follow the rest.

Chelsea Butler
Millside School - Haybrook College, Slough

Polar Bears

You come and kill us
Please don't kill us.

Help me, I'm dying!
I wish I could shoot you.

I'm lonely 'cause my mum and dad are dead
Humans killed them.

I'm tired and hungry, give me some fish
No, you won't let me eat.

You are human
You aren't nice.

You will kill all of us
And sell our skins.

I'd like to sell your skin
And put you in the bin.

Mikey Hoad
Millside School - Haybrook College, Slough

I Am The Knuckles Of Harry's Hand

Harry's knuckles, they feel the pain
When Harry's temper is put under strain
He gets angry and hits a wall
Why can't he just hit a ball?
I know they feel like they are taken for granted
But they are becoming incredibly slanted.
He cracks them daily to release the air
But he's the one that causes them despair.

Harry Hewett
Millside School - Haybrook College, Slough

David Attenborough

You tried to influence the world
Your ideas seemed very bold
You have to be consistent
And have to do it quickly,
'Cause you're getting a bit sickly.
You also find it tricky
'Cause you like to do documentaries
About the world's animals who are sickly
And dying because of us.

Taylor Stevens
Millside School - Haybrook College, Slough

Not Just A Condition

I have a condition,
One that means I am small,
Achondroplasia is what it is called.

I thought I couldn't do anything,
Then I met sport,
One that I knew I would love.

Only the age of five,
I was already a professional,
Taking my mind off myself,
My dejected heart couldn't believe it,
I finally found something that I loved.

Because of this activity,
I didn't care what people thought,
I didn't care about the future,
I cared about now.

I was entered into a competition,
One for kids with disabilities,
One made for me,
A wave of happiness came over me,
I felt like I was at home,
I fitted in so well.

In the changing room, my heart was pounding,
Thump,
Thump,

Thump,
Thump,
Stretching my goggles over my head,
I can do this,
My inner voice whispered with motivation.

Then it was my time to shine,
My time to show everyone,
Just because I was small,
It didn't mean that I couldn't do anything.

I lowered myself into the pool,
The cold, refreshing water relieved me,
I took deep breaths,
In,
Out,
In,
Out.

The klaxon sounded,
I was off,
As fast as I could go,
Before I knew it,
I had won!
I was so proud.

Next stop, Beijing!
Paralympics, here I come,
Thirteen years of age,

So young,
I was here,
Already.

My dream came true,
Up against,
Some of my heroes,
Two races,
I couldn't win them.

Nerve-racking moment,
Who would win?
"The winner of the 100m and 400m freestyle is..."
The commentator announced,
I couldn't believe it,
I had won,
Both,
Two gold medals.

Next year,
Training,
Training,
Training,
Competitions, here I come!

A letter in the post,
I was off to London,
To receive an important award,
Only an MBE!

At fourteen years,
The youngest ever to get it,
I was grateful,
I was thankful,
I was proud,
Never in a million years would I have ever thought of meeting the Queen,
Let alone receive an MBE.

Every four years for the rest of my life,
I was in different countries,
Against different people,
Medals, medals, medals,
That's what I was known for,
Clink!
Clink!
My pieces of gold went.

Britain's golden girl,
That's me!
Small but feisty,
That's me.
Proud of what I've achieved,
That's me.

Hana Rashid (12)
President Kennedy School, Holbrooks

Florence Nightingale

Born in May 1820
Grew up in Italy eating penne
I have one older sibling
Always having to do her bidding
I'm one of the wealthiest
But that won't stop me being the friendliest
Although I was never the best at socialising
Maybe because Mother was quite patronising
Our mother and daughter relationship was never the best
She would constantly compare me to the rest
Now 1836 is the year
It's God's voice I seem to hear
Telling me that I ought to be
A nurse, helping ones unlike me
It's time to make a confession
I want nursing to be my profession
Just as I thought, Mother and Father are not amused
Now I am the one who is being accused
Hate forbids me to achieve
My one and only magical dream
1853
Oh no! The Crimean War has broken out!
And our lives are at stake
Fear not, for peace will save the day
Now I am working all the time
I have to admit, it feels divine

To know that I am doing God's work
For it is God I'm trying to serve
They call me The Lady with the Lamp
For at night, I nurse the soldiers in their camp
Now I'm the first woman doctor
I could not be prouder
I've opened up a clinic
And helped poor people in it
The soldiers appreciate me
Being the best nurse I can be
Now I've opened up a school
Following the medical rule
More people are becoming like me
Now they are beginning to see
Women can achieve the best
But there is no time for rest
Now we all stand united
Come on, women, you're all invited
I do God's work for a great cause
I try to achieve it with no flaws
I've even published a book
So everyone can look
At the work I've produced
And the new hygiene levels I've introduced
My work here has been done.

At the ripe old age of ninety
Florence Nightengale died feeling mighty

Her work is still remembered today
As The Lady with the Lamp who had her say.

Maab Hejaaji (11)
President Kennedy School, Holbrooks

Treatment After Treatment

I fought the battle and won,
But here I am once again, going through the same treatment,
One thing my nurse told me was that it would be the end of my treatment one day,
And it was, until the dreaded doctor's appointment.

I remember ringing the bell when I was just seven,
And now, just five years later, it's happening again,
My first chemotherapy in five years is coming up soon,
I tried to procrastinate the thought of me going through the pain again,
But it's true, it is going to happen, and I am going to face the truth,
Everything I ever worked for to be healthy again has been thrown away,
Or, at least, that's what it feels like.

My nurse always told me to be brave, but I don't know if I can,
I don't know if I'm strong enough to survive the second time.
I can't throw away my family and lose everyone important in my life,
I must fight another treatment,
Another suffering for the people I cherish the most,
I will fight and I will survive as well as I did before.
I will fight the battle, and I will win!

Tayla-Louise Wing (12)
President Kennedy School, Holbrooks

Living The Dream

I remember sitting in my room on the dirty floor
Staring at my faded posters
Zidane, Figo and many more
And wondering how it would be
To be living the dream.

I remember hiding in my room
Listening to the drunken shouts
Hiding from my father
Over me and my mother, he would loom
Living in poverty is not easy.

I remember begging for food
Shivering, tired, half-nude
Only to be turned down
And wondering, something that I know now
What it would be like to be living the dream.

I remember turning up for training
Being bullied and mocked by my teammates
Almost physically fighting
And thinking bitterly
How I was not taking it easy.

I remember playing my first match
Dribbling and shooting
My teammates watched in awe
At the match's end, their faces were filled

With newfound respect
And thinking
This is what it must be like
To be living the dream.

Now I sit here
Resting on my trophies
The best player in the world
And I think
Now I know what it's like
To be living the dream.

Milo Shakespeare (11)
President Kennedy School, Holbrooks

A Daily Struggle

Thump-thump.
Thump-thump.
"Just breathe," they say.
But I can't.
"It's fine," they say.
But it isn't.
It will never be fine, not ever.
I'm panic-stricken and helpless.
The oxygen is being sucked out from deep within my lungs.
The world is crumbling around me like an avalanche of darkness.
I drop to the floor.
I'm seeing stars.
Too much to handle, too much to bear.
It is over, nothing matters.
Suffocation; my worst enemy: myself.
When I look at my reflection,
A girl,
Not who I am, but what others see.
A mask, a shield, my protection.
If only that mirror could read into my heart,
Uncover the broken shards of my soul.
It would reveal the true story.
Struggle, but also hope.
There is much struggle.
Struggle to withhold this mask.

Struggle to contain emotions.
Struggle to never let this smile waver.
But there is also hope.
Hope to remove this mask.
Let these emotions fly free.
And hope to smile. But to really mean it.

Perhaps there will always be struggle.
A constant shadow looming over me.
And there will always be problems.
Challenges to test my resilience.
But hope is always welcome,
A friend I never knew I could have.

Lara Krefta (12)
President Kennedy School, Holbrooks

Knife Angel

Even after all the begging,
You all still ignore me,
If only if I could,
I really would,
Beg on my knees.

Some might be resting,
Some might be bathing,
Or they might be,
They just might be,
Getting ready for their unnecessary role,
Their unnecessary acts,
Their time to shine,
And find the dark hole everyone needs to experience.

These hideous actions make me cry,
Because all these innocent people will have to die.
Sadly, life isn't fair,
But I know some of you might care.

Endless praying,
Endless murders,
Endless crying,
Endless pain,
If I could,
I would,
Stop this endless nightmare.

Some people will cry,
Others will feel power now,
Seeing others die.

If I could,
I would,
Beg for your help.

Day by day, night by night,
People look up to me,
Realising all these mistakes,
Finally, they notice what reality is,
And my praying shall not go to waste.

Still, today, I await,
For something marvellous to arrive,
Even though I know,
It never will.

Shanuja Elangeswaran (11)
President Kennedy School, Holbrooks

Champions League

Looking back, it only seemed like yesterday,
But it was fifteen years ago.
There I sat on the bench, twitching,
I was as excited as I was nervous.
Crazy thoughts ran through my mind,
Like an athlete completing a marathon.
I was only seventeen at the time,
I felt like a little boy playing with men.
At that age, I could never have thought about playing for the biggest team,
However, there I was, warming up to get substituted on.
As soon as I stepped on the pitch, the atmosphere was electric,
As if sparks were running from the pitch, through my boots and into my veins.
One hundred thousand people glaring at me,
One hundred thousand people I could show my skills to.
I came on the pitch with eight minutes to go.
It only felt like eight seconds when I heard the final whistle blow.
Throughout all of my achievements, the trophies and goals,
The memories of this night are my biggest treasure.

Ellis James Harridence (11)
President Kennedy School, Holbrooks

Mental Health

I go insane as I try to close my eyes,
I want to help, but no one listens to my cries,
The paramedics give me advice,
The voice inside my head, a plan it has devised.

Keeping me awake during the winter nights,
It's cold, the strange voices enjoying my frights,
The feeling, the scare thumps inside my head,
I've gone out of my mind, my heart's stopped dead.

No one will hear me cry out my sorrow,
My heart is crying out as it's sad, hollow,
Mourning my soul of sadness and despair,
My mind has no more thoughts, it's just a cloud, air.

The paramedics trying to help me calm down,
My mind is empty, no thoughts to be shared, it's like a cloud.
My mind's printing off thoughts, running out of ideas,
Rolling down my cheeks are droplets of water, tears.

Abbie Clarke (11)
President Kennedy School, Holbrooks

Nelson Mandela: The Hero Of A Lifetime

Born in 1918 in South Africa,
To spend twenty-seven years in prison,
He must have had some stamina.

He stood up for black people's rights,
This must have caused some sleepless nights.

Nelson Mandela joined the ANC (African National Congress) in 1944,
Striving for equal rights,
Trying to change the law.

ANC was banned by the white government,
As a crowd of people were on the hunt,
Mandela didn't like what they had done,
So in his memory, he thought he had won.

Arrested for leaving the country on the 5th of August, 1962,
With no other option, what else was there for him to do?

Released in 1990, the people of South Africa cheered,
When they saw that Nelson Mandela was free and appeared.

Ethan Moore (11)
President Kennedy School, Holbrooks

Plastic

When I'm washing up on your sandy beaches,
I'm choking on plastic coated in your oily slimes,
My waves may seem majestic at first,
But they do not display a healthy, clear sea,
You humans just don't care,
Plastic packaging and plastic rings,
Plastic bags for more plastic things,
Plastic bottles for the water you drink,
The more you do this,
The less I have to live,
Plastic thrown away and out of reach,
Ends up as plastic on a plastic beach,
Yet, you don't see this,
Do you?
Millions of sea birds and turtles painfully die,
And it's all because of you,
You poisoned me,
You killed me,
And you will be the ones that end up without me.

Isabelle May Betts (12)
President Kennedy School, Holbrooks

Deforestation

They burn us, torture us,
I have to watch my brothers die beside me,
I cannot help them, we are all defenceless,
While we are stuck to the ground, they take our lives viciously,
Monkeys swing from branch to branch, but soon their homes will be destroyed,
They come closer to me,
Fear is rising within me,
Blankets of red make their way closer and closer to me,
All animals are fleeing,
I know they're coming for me,
I feel the heat to my right,
They're here,
Pain engulfs me,
I feel chopping,
What have I done to deserve this?
I try to cling on,
It is no use,
I'm falling,
They've taken me,
This is where I end.

Shiv Nagra (11)
President Kennedy School, Holbrooks

The Sweet Dream For Dance

Nothing matters when I begin,
My dreams melt into a reality,
Soft, buttery and sweet,
The music absorbs me, sweeping me into a faraway fairy tale,
I stretch, twirl and leap,
I pirouette and spin,
Please let this sweet confectionary tale never end,
I feel my heart pulse along my chest, almost dancing to the same rhythm I feel,
Pure joy, pure contentment,
I feel the ache in my muscles,
The contentment begins to fade,
The music stops, its rhythm like watercolour fading away,
I open my eyes and I'm faced with reality,
The clapping begins and the cheering becomes a silent drum in the background,
Dancing is my life,
Dancing is my passion.

Kristina Popovic (11)
President Kennedy School, Holbrooks

My Secret Crush

At you, I keep on staring,
Will I be so daring?
To talk to you one day,
But I don't know what to say.
You have no idea, you have no clue,
How much I think of you.
My heart you steal,
Will you ever ask me out to a meal?
We started talking,
I went red,
Without you, I would be dead.
I tell my mate,
They think it's a mistake.
I think it's the wrong decision,
I'm in a bad position.
The next day, catastrophe!
All my friends running after me,
Asking if it's true,
Why do they doubt my love for you?
From day one, you had my heart,
I wish we could restart.
This poem is for you.

Ameera Bawazir (11)
President Kennedy School, Holbrooks

Monster High School

Dear Diary,
I am Flora Evergreen.
Finally, a place where
my words don't fall on deaf ears.

I walk down these crowded halls
where shadows torment me.
Their grins growing wider
for my existing fear.

Friends follow me
to suck my life out of my belly.
Their fangs are bared
I wonder how long they'll be...

My true friends are
in the hands of corruption
of the women who lure with songs
and broken hearts crash into their islands of lies.

I tried so many times
with the loop inside the rope
because who can hear a cry whose mouth is cut?
The tongue of a helpless person.

Cailey Rushton (11)
President Kennedy School, Holbrooks

Through Her Eyes

For me, life was missing its colours,
But what would it be without the ups and downs?
It's what holds us from breaking apart,
Breaking into a million pieces.

An electricity bolt took the life of the person I had loved the most,
Who was she to me? That, I'll never know.
Life is never complete without the love you need,
But it's never easy to move on.

It was only a matter of time before I could move on,
But could I really?
I moved away and began a life of my own,
All the love I needed was there,
But when the last rose blooms, my new life will begin.

Inaya Ratiq (11)
President Kennedy School, Holbrooks

The Unknown

Am I a prisoner being hunted by the military?
Am I a human with unique features?
Am I an animal that can't move?
Who am I?
Am I a forest that has been brutalised by humans?
Am I a book with powers no living being can dream of having?
Am I a triangle without three sides?
Who am I?
Am I a computer without a monitor?
Am I a window without glass?
Am I a piece of chocolate that has been chucked in the bin?
What am I?

Diwan Kadr (11)
President Kennedy School, Holbrooks

Forest Tribesmen

Dear Mr Bolsonaro,
why are there machines in my home?
Tearing up my village,
and the rainforest too.

I lived a peaceful life,
gathering berries and hunting,
living in my forest,
the leaves were my bunting.

Dear Mr Tribesman,
my people look to me,
to end their suffering,
poverty and crime.
I cannot give them what they want,
unless I use the forest,
a cache of resources best used,
to fill their empty stomachs.

Until my people have a life,
the forest is their saviour,
food and homes and work,
medicine too.

You can have your forest when we're done,
I am sure it will be soon,
until then, there is nothing I can do.

Dear Mr Bolsonaro,
that's not good enough.
If your people lived like me,
this problem would be solved.
They could live amongst the trees,
hunter-gatherer tribes,
then we can have our forest,
and they can have their lives.

You may not listen to me here,
I accept it may be true,
but listen to others who shout my plea,
shout it right at you.

Look at all those children striking in the streets,
this is who they want to help,
forest tribes like me.

If you will continue,
and really will not stop,
then I will fight to live my life,
in a forest.

If a dead land is your dream,
then really kill me now.
I would rather die,
than live in a world,
where a forest has no trees.

Seren Jones
Priory School, Southsea

Trapped

I'm trapped.
Trapped in the cage of my mind,
Spiralling, spiralling, spiralling,
Falling into the dark thoughts that await.
They don't like me - none of them do.
I'm just that lonely freak who mutters to herself in the corner;
Crying, screaming, rocking back and forth,
Watching chunks of hair fall to the floor.
They're out to get me, I swear.
They're plotting against me.
I have no purpose here -
Let me go, go, go!
Tears splash to the ground,
Images flashing through my head: pointing, jeering, blade, mocking, sneering, knife, laughing...
Knife.
Shaky breaths tumbling over each other, fighting to get out first,
Fighting like the thoughts in my head:
Take it!
I can't!
You have no purpose on this Earth anyway.
They'll miss me!
Who will? Nobody likes you.
Footsteps pounding, brow dappled with sweat,

Steel blade glinting in the feverish light.
I'm a bird, enclosed in my cage,
A dove willing for peace.
Let it free, let it out - turn the key,
Behind those nightmares must be something good.
A beautiful creature, seeking its future somewhere else...
Gone.

Marianne Grace McIntyre (11)
Priory School, Southsea

Why Do You Hate Me?

Why do you hate me?
I just don't understand
When I'm watching the news
My eyes fixated on you
Don't you think I wonder who
Has spoken this gossip?
It's not true!
Even when you say I've lied
I don't sit on my bed and sigh
Wondering why the whole world hates me
Even though all I've done is try
Tears still fill my very eyes
And I try my hardest not to cry
What would you do if you were the president
And I was simply just a resident?
Would you plea for peace and harmony
Just like me?
I have tried my hardest to get to the top
But all you want to do is make me stop
I am not an alien from Mars
I know how to drive a car
All I want is for you to remember
Even up until the next December
When you watch the fake news
Don't believe that it's all true
Stop tagging alongside the crowd

And be your own individual
Make yourself proud
Shout out loud!
Why do you hate me?
Aren't I like you?
Aren't you like me?
We are one, aren't we?
Don't judge a book by its cover...

Jasmine Georgy (11)
Queen Elizabeth's Grammar School, Blackburn

Through Their Eyes

Through their eyes, they live in a palace of gold,
Their crowns sit gleaming on their heads.
They slay mighty dragons and attend stunning masquerade balls,
They live a life of luxury.

Through their eyes, they are famous explorers,
They travel to every corner of the world.
They meet wild animals and find treasure in an abandoned tomb,
Their lives are never boring.

Through their eyes, they shoot off in a rocket to space,
They explore the shining stars.
They walk on the moon and cross the furthest of galaxies,
They never want to come down.

But.

Through my eyes, I see the peeling wallpaper,
I smell the mould from the roof.
I can see the landlord wanting his monthly rent that I don't have,
I see all the problems they don't.

Through my eyes, I see our bank account,
The number is scarily low.
I hoped I could afford to give them a better future,
But I see the truth.

Through my eyes, our lives are dreadful,
I have no one to turn to.
I want to fly and escape this life, but I'm caged to reality,
I see that we are trapped.

I wish I could see through their eyes,
Live with that child-like innocence.
But I am here and that won't change,
So I must keep going...

Victoria Wreford (16)
Richard Taunton Sixth Form College, Southampton

Steeling Lives

All I see is death,
All I smell is blood.

Everywhere I turn,
There is nothing to earn.

I am gripped and slashed,
And thrown around.

I am in and out of bodies,
I have been in many.

Yet I have touched no lives,
But taken many away.

There are many bad things,
That me and my master have done.

None of these deeds I am proud of,
But there are still more to come.

It is coming closer to my time,
I have become restless and rusty.

But during my life of stainless steel,
I have harmed many.

Have brought no goodness,
And have killed hundreds.

Rhiannon Natalya Kimber (16)
Richard Taunton Sixth Form College, Southampton

10v3r

His voice,
It echoes in my head
Even with the bass of the speakers
Blaring on.

This place,
It's too small for us both,
He knows I love a stadium,
Not this.

I'm fragile:
One drop of any drink
And I'm gone. But here,
I am proud.

I am his.
With his hand around my waist,
He gives me a gentle squeeze,
And sings.

Ben Jefferis (17)
Richard Taunton Sixth Form College, Southampton

Life Is A Struggle

Racism can be casual or come in massive flurries,
Filling your mind with insecurities but also tremendous worries.
Lots of idols have changed the world and stopped racial discrimination,
But also strife, being scared and being filled with humiliation.
There aren't many ethnics in this specific place,
Personally, I think all the racists should deserve to feel disgrace.
Right now, we stand on a planet where the aura is dark,
But there are quite a few people who have made their mark.

Rosa Parks is a fantastic person whose spirit will never diminish,
But we will mostly remember her for her attempt to stand up.
She marched up and down the streets, accomplishing a significant part of history,
However, we do not know how or when racism will end, I guess it's a mystery.
She is most famous for sitting down on the bus,
Making a statement to the whites and achieving for us.
It shouldn't happen, that's why we make a fuss.

Around here is very different from my previous accommodation,
A lot of white people and a lot of complications.

I ask...
Why can't everyone just get along?
It will be a long time until it's like where I'm from.
I think everyone should settle down,
It doesn't matter whether you're white, black or brown...
It shouldn't happen!

Martin Luther was certainly a king,
Due to all the ideas and amazement he tried to bring.
To a racist world full of absolute ignorance,
A dream he had, but he received intolerance,
Shot down for his thoughts,
Where the white disagreed and fought.
Moreover, he was an extravagant man,
Who stood up for his beliefs with an astonishing plan!

When I was about four, I was excluded from every event,
At that age, I didn't know exactly what this meant.
So from that day on, I built a wall of immunity,
Towards the racism I received from the community.
The moral of this poem...
Racism is unacceptable, everyone is just as important
And racism needs some powerful reinforcement.
As we all know, the Black History Month is October,
I just hope to see the world one time when it's sober...
Of racism.

Trevane Dante Winditt (13)
Somervale School, Midsomer Norton

Am I Good Enough?

Am I good enough?
When I asked myself, "Am I good enough?"
I was feeling so blue.
My friends turned on me.
I had no clue what to do.
My mind was a mess.
I was really depressed.
I could never express... how I truly felt.
Am I good enough, am I good enough, am I good enough?
Hiding inside my bedsheet, I cried my eyes out.
But then something came to my head.
I am good enough!
No one can tell me I am not.
I am me.
And me is me.
I can't change who I am.
I am happy with me.
I will be me forever, so I might as well get used to it.
I am happy in my body.
And that is final.

Aoife Duggan-Lee
Somervale School, Midsomer Norton

Nature's Truth

My story is a lie,
But the lie is never ever shared,
That corrupts me in my sleep,
The death, the hatred,
My eyes, heartbeat.
My shallow eye,
Dive deep like a deep ocean beat,
Like a crow croaking, like a lion meows,
A sweet rose bleeding for their life's new nature,
My death changes to the light never-ending,
My sorrowful heart cries to my beating breath.

Katie Marie Smith (13)
Somervale School, Midsomer Norton

All About Me

If my life was made into a story
and you read it
you would probably get bored
in about two minutes
but I don't care
because
it is my life
not anyone else's
and
I don't care
if anyone else thinks
I'm boring
or
uncool
because
I know
I
am
not
and
it only matters
what I think
because
I
am
the most interesting person in the world.

Ryan Hitchens (11)
Somervale School, Midsomer Norton

Myself

Pink dresses and sparkly heels,
Um, no thanks.
Hoodies and joggers,
Yes please.

Fancy food and an orange juice mocktail,
No thanks.
Chicken nuggets on the sofa with a Diet Coke?
Yes please.

Having people over late at night for a party?
No thanks.
Chill, eat food and watch Netflix?
Yes please.

Izabella Gardiner
Somervale School, Midsomer Norton

A Ruler Of The Sea

In the land of legend, there is a sea which I rule
It's filled with great wonder and I get to rule it all
Of all the creatures in my kingdom, I am by far most exotic
So powerful, in fact, I could even turn demonic.

Many of the noble towns will be engulfed by the crimson sea
They will lie still and untouched for all of eternity
As the landscape around them will crumble as sorrow leaks in
I will go scavenging the ruins, killing any remaining survivors to rid them of sin.

The humans of this graceful planet decide to take their last stand
But in the end, they are not enough and always need a hand
This is because the crimson sea corrupts all beings
It turns the most peaceful of creatures into monsters and rids them of feelings.

However, despite my size and all this time, no one has ever caught a glimpse of me
Why?
As every lucky soul who sees me ends up dead to some degree
So I'll tell you my secret of what I am
I am the Kraken and in the end, all shall end up damned.

Alfie Taylor (11)
St Aidan's CE Academy, Darlington

Gaia

Every day, my condition worsens,
It won't be long before it ends.
Over and over, they say they'll help,
Though they'll never overcome their unconscious greed.

They look at me and all they see,
Is a chance for exploitation.
Though you take me for granted,
My presence is not eternal.

Once I'm gone, they'll finally learn,
But soon, it'll be too late.
Though, I cannot complain,
For soon, there will be eternal peace.

Lily Potter (11)
St Aidan's CE Academy, Darlington

Heading Home

Travelling through the sky,
Day in,
Day out,
Never stopping,
As we fly north.

As we leave the snow behind,
We travel to a distant land.
Arriving in the warmth of Canada,
We settle and breed.

Mollie Pinkney (11)
St Aidan's CE Academy, Darlington

Nature's Cry

When your kind first walked on this land,
My brethren and I offered our branches as shelter,
And our fruits as nourishment.
As we grew, you did the same,
And for a while, we lived in perfect balance.
But no matter how wise I become,
I shall never understand why your kind,
Began slaughtering us for your own benefit.

Now, my brothers are dead.

We had a few creatures who loved us and swung from our branches, but,
I assume, out of jealousy, you killed them too.
Now, I stand alone in these barren wastelands,
Dying much slower than my brothers.
You no longer eat of my fruit as I have none to give,
Instead, you carve your names into me,
Like a farmer brands his cattle.

However, we will recover,
Of this, I am certain.
Your kind will die as a result of your own sins,
And our kind will reclaim the lands we once ruled.
There isn't much that humours me now,
But the knowledge that you will feed us,
The very beings you spent your lives destroying,
Makes my old soul smile.

Abigail Eve Donlon (17)
St John Rigby College, Orrell

Beautiful Kings

Chasing. Charging. Coursing. Hunting.
It's what I do best, this game of cat and mouse,
For I am the cat and I want to play.

My mouse hurries along with its long legs flailing,
I smile, for my legs are longer.
My mouse careens around a corner, teeth bared in desperation,
I grin, for my teeth are sharper.
My mouse hides, soft flanks shadowed by undergrowth,
I laugh, for I am the shadow.

Slash. Shred. Sever. Hunted.
I retire to my palace, a place of forgotten power.
A king rules where a king once ruled,
His story is legendary, as is mine.
Those who sheltered began to show, rising up to him.
Taken for granted, the king died.

I, the Once and Future King, lazily stroll and saunter,
My kingdom quiet, sleeping, still.
Camouflaged in orange and black, I melt away into the thick forest,
At ease, surrounded by my home, my heart.
That stillness lasts - until it doesn't.

I see, but am sighted.
I hear, but am heard.

I trap, but am trapped.
I wound, but am wounded.
What dares question the cat?
Hunter: humans.

I am not the king.
They are.

Holly Fairhurst (16)
St John Rigby College, Orrell

They Built Me A Face

Limestone arches, reaching and falling like one eyebrow to another.
They bolt upright, hovering hope in dome,
Before diving down, grounded to a concrete certainty.

Between,
They fitted some glass shards to peer through,
But my view was already tinted, staining the brilliant light,
Drowning all those who came to hear with vicious cardinal,
Like the red sea overwhelming their lungs,
Taking each breath and filling it, infiltrating salt and broken shells,
Shells where life once dwelled.

Fragments carefully composed feign saviours lamenting their griefs.
Offering my solace to the junkies seeking release,
A granite mouth they engraved for me where my soul was to be,
Cut into morsels, altered and thrust down the throats of the hungry,
A place to declare diatribes, impudent and lucid.

Candelabrums strike upwards, pinching a fickle fire,
Wax streams until... still.
It wobbles, clotting in a heavy drip on the lip of my decree.
"All rise."

Heather Ann Tully-Bolton (16)
St John Rigby College, Orrell

Two Toffs In A Tower

The 'good old grab 'n' go' we calls it
or a 'smash 'n' dash', but less of that,
'cause a constable'll catch you for all the noise.
A 'rough 'n' tumble' is the neighbour's word -
neighbours is always old folks in gowns
and lanterns, long, pokey noses, asking,
"Who's you?"
"What's the noise?"
and, the one we hates,
"Show us the bag, then," before they call
and every bobby from Palace to Greens comes running;
all for some old fogies shouting
and clattering of the nag's hooves on cobble wakes the rest up.
But we has our 'funs 'n' runs' before they gets us,
finding our own cab, hailing the driver,
"How much to Bottom's End?"
and he says, "Only a tuppence,"
so we trundle away on the pea-soup-express,
safe as two toffs in a tower.

Oskar Leonard (16)
St John Rigby College, Orrell

The Fool's Love

The way I dance and throw myself to ropes,
Amongst the clouds of seats and bags of light,
The way I juggle with beams of lights and hopes,
With many o' eyes with me directly in sight.

I balance, I tussle, I fiddle, I struggle with glee,
Knowing full well that all of the attention,
Will finally, tonight, be laid into me,
And through their stares, I feel a connection.

But those connections were those of hateful glares,
Engravements of fury and much disdain,
With echoes of heckles, they threw their shares,
Causing my bouncing soul to stand still in pain.

Although I'd love to perform a longer while,
The love I have for the stage is enough to make me smile.

Caner Aydin (16)
St John Rigby College, Orrell

Through The Eyes Of A Newborn Baby

My eyes opened and my life began.
I saw faces I would love, respect and trust forever.
Through their eyes, I could see knowledge and experience;
I longed to learn from them.
I felt love seeping from their every pore.
I felt hugs and kisses smothering me
But I felt safe and loved.
I learnt to cry when I needed something;
I couldn't yet speak.
I cried when I was hungry, tired or cold or just needed to be loved.
Whatever the time of day or night, I knew that I would be comforted.
I slept peacefully with nothing to fear.
No worries did I have; I knew they were there for me.
The faces smiled down upon me, happy, but sometimes tired.
I knew that I was not alone and that I never would be.
It was the beginning of my life, but I knew that it would be a great one.

Milvydas Sadauskas (12)
St John's Catholic Comprehensive School, Gravesend

Football Madness

F IFA champions
O bviously cool teams
O ctober football seasons
T raining on the moon
B alls bounce and slide
A lways love football
L iverpool are rubbish
L osers and winners.

P remier League football
R oma are the best team!
O bviously, I am the best footballer you'll ever see!

Brodie Lynch (11)
St John's Catholic Comprehensive School, Gravesend

Home

There was a time I used
To look into my father's eyes
In a happy place where I could
Call it my home
Then someone had to go
And time went so slow
I hear the songs from my
Primary years ago
Upon the lies that I've been told
I've never met someone that cold
I remember how it all came
I was never the same.

Jeena Bhanot (12)
St John's Catholic Comprehensive School, Gravesend

Constantly Running, Running For Another Day

I lost everything and everyone, they took everything we loved
For me it was my family.
I travelled across the world, my greatest fear
But I must be here for what had happened last year.

I'm now in America trying to get into university,
I have seen all of the different people,
I now know the meaning of diversity,
I like it but the people don't.
Well, they don't like me,
They don't like me and my people,
Because of my beliefs,
Because I am a Muslim.

People are chasing me, I'm running down the street,
I don't know where I'm going but I know it's an endless place,
I have to keep up the pace, it feels like a game,
More like a race.
I have to get to the finish line before them,
But there is no line.
I keep going and going every single day,
I'm constantly running, running for another day.

Waking up to daylight was the first fun thing to do
But now I'm scared, it's like a nightmare for me to do.
I can't face these people waiting for me
Outside my house,
This is insane
Just because of who I am, I have to go through this pain.

People are chasing me, I'm running down the street,
I don't know where I'm going but I know it's an endless place,
I have to keep up the pace, it feels like a game,
More like a race.
I have to get to the finish line before them,
But there is no line.
I keep going and going every single day,
I'm constantly running, running for another day.

Now here comes May,
The month I came here and where it all began.
Now it's the month where it all will end,
I'm now happy again to see the sunrise,
A message I will send
Before I die.
I get out my house and see the same people,
Instead of running, I stand still,
I smile and say,
"Why should I be constantly running?"
They get me, they beat me, they make sure blood comes out of me, they rob me...

They find nothing apart from the note I wrote saying...

'What have I done? My name is Abdullah,
I came here hoping for nothing but peace,
But I got the opposite...
Are you doing this because one of my kind killed someone?
Did a terrorist attack somewhere? Rob someone? So?
How and why does this mean every single one of us is bad people?
My whole family died because of you.
It's the same thing but I know all of you aren't bad...
Why should we be constantly running, running for another day?'
I want all of you to remember
I want all of you to be a member
A member of the anti-Islamophobia
Remember that we aren't all bad people
There is half of everything like how there are half bad and good people.

Anjali Banger (12)
Villiers High School, Southall

A Stop To Knife Crime

Mum's crying, shedding tears
Son's dying, showed no fear
Killers silenced, court they fear
What future do they have in a cell? That's clear.

Football's a gift, it doesn't just come
Act who you are, don't be dumb
Know who you are and know what you've done
You've taken a life, that's somebody's son.

What would you do if he was yours?
Killer showing no remorse
Every day you cry to sleep
Because someone went to act like a sheep
Yes, we know he was your son
100% innocent, nothing done wrong.

Something that's wrong is that he's not here
And his mother and father are shedding tears
Knife crime's not a joke, it really isn't a game
Since the early 2000s the streets haven't been safe
So be aware and be careful of all your surroundings
And think before you make another mother shed a fountain.

Only thirteen, you think you're running the street
Carrying knives, parents scared.

Ayuub Siad (14)
Villiers High School, Southall

Hidden Behind A Smile

When happiness has turned its back
and your heart's about to break,
I'll trickle down your cheek,
not a noise shall I make.
You try and hold me back
but I shall break free.
I'll leave your sticky prison;
captivity isn't for me.
You're ashamed that I've escaped,
you try and hold me in,
I don't think anyone's told you
crying isn't a sin.
You hide me behind a smile,
while the sadness grows and grows.
People tease and sneer
but nobody really knows
that I'm hiding here
itching to go.

For I am your tears
the one and only thing
that sees how bad the jeers really sting.
Each of them like an arrow to your heart,
shot by people who think they're smart.
Can't they see that behind your smile
I'm held contained at least for a little while...
The thing is everyone thinks I'm here to add a sad touch

but sometimes, on a good day
you'll smile so much
that you'll feel happy in every way,
that's when I'll come racing down your cheek,
I won't be held back nor restrained,
for this time you don't want to hold back the leak
and you let me fall not at all ashamed.

I am the very thing that reflects your inner thoughts
because sometimes words are just not enough.
Whether you're happy or sad,
I'll be with you through the smooth and rough.
Falling gently from your face,
I am the one thing that cannot be held back whatever the case.
So through your emotions I shall come,
wiped away by the back of your thumb.

Sanika Kiritharan (12)
Villiers High School, Southall

Mother

I've been waiting for a long time
For you to appear
Tell me, is it a crime
Wishing that you were here?
We may be miles apart
Yet it feels as if you are near
I can never forget you
As you are my mother dear.

Father may have left
He told that I should join you
There is this heavy weight on my chest
Asking me why I feel so blue
I have many sisters and brothers
Their love for me is strong
They love me like no other
I'm certain that this can't go wrong.

Mother, I feel like I'm on top of the world
When I'm certain that you're the one I love
I'm pretty sure you know this
As you are always watching from above
You taught me right and you taught me wrong
Without you, I'll be on my own
No matter where you are,
I know I love you to the bone.

I'm an orphan, no one loves me,
I used to think
Then I realised, you are always in my heart
And my love will never shrink
I know that I'm weak
But one thing's for sure
That one day I will become stronger
And become so much more.

People come and people go
But parents stay the same till the end
That's the one thing that I don't have
Friendship is important, as if they are broken, it's hard to mend
Before I was lonely and now, I have friends
They love me for who I am
Even if we fight, we make amends
One thing is for sure
No one's a greater friend than you, Mother.

Mathusha Vijayarasa (12)
Villiers High School, Southall

Mum For Life!

Is she Mum or God?
Because the way she acts,
Is like a goddess.
Mother is such a simple word,
But there's a big meaning,
Behind the word mother.

Nobody's equal to my mum,
Not even God,
I'm blessed by God,
To have a mum like her.

Even though she is always,
Shouting at me,
And is always stressing me out,
This is what I've become,
A very successful student,
But still, I am stressed.

Still stressed about what?
What I have done for my mum.
Am I stressed,
Or have I made my mum stressed?

She is always like, "Jaskaran, do this,
Jaskaran, do that!"
Then, when I rest for a bit,
She is like,

"Go do something!"

Mum, Mum,
She is always making me feel yum,
She made me not dumb,
And when I'm done with everything,
She is always making sure,
I have fun.

Oh Mum, oh Mum,
What would I have done without you?
Would I be as smart as I am?
Would I be having tasty food?
Would I be doing work?
Would I be having fun?

Mum, you are my pain,
But at the same time, you are my hope,
Are you a villain or a hero?
Because what you have done for me,
You even have done greater than a hero!
Mum, you are the nicest thing I have ever wished for,
I love you, Mum,
Mum for life!

Jaskaran Singh Lamba (11)
Villiers High School, Southall

My Best Diwali

So excited, it's soon Diwali,
We've had and will have even more fun with our friends and families,
It's always been beautiful,
And it always makes our year pass through happily.

The festival of light and colour,
Every year, there are new things to discover.
The festival of Rama and Sita, where we all light fireworks,
Diwali comes in winter, why not summer?

Celebrating with my mother and father.
While decorating, houses get brighter and brighter.
Cleaning our houses from every corner,
Making rangolis from the front of the house to the back with lots of laughter.

Doing the aartis and the poojas, worshipping God,
Spending, with our relatives, all the time we can
Welcoming Rama and Sita through the front porch,
Explaining to the children to not be naughty, but good.

Sharing out sweets and presents,
Sharing love with your parents.
Do the best to cheer everyone up,
Doing sparklers and fun snaps with the family members.

Getting new clothes and accessories to dress up on the day,
To get the right one, trying out hairstyles every day,

Helping relatives get what they need,
Lighting divas and candles, especially in the doorways.

Prisha Prisha (11)
Villiers High School, Southall

Dreams

You want a big house, many cars and wealth
but actually you don't have any dreams.

You live quite comfortably, even if you don't dream
no one says anything.
Everyone is thinking the same way as you.
You completely forget the days when you had dreams.

What is it that you dream of?
Who do you see in the mirror?
Who do you want to be?
Go on your path, even if you live for a day.
Do something and put away your weakness
and go and achieve your dreams.

Stop! Ask yourself if you have ever
worked hard for anything.
Why are you telling yourself to go
and take a different path?
Take care of yourself.
Don't force away all your dreams.

Rebel against the hell-like society
Dreams are a special part of your game
Ask yourself about your dream profile
Become the main subject of your life
That has always been suppressed because of your dreams.

You don't know how to live
You don't know how to fly
You don't know how to decide
You don't know how to dream
Stop hesitating, stop being indecisive
Open your eyes now, dream a dream now
And decide what you dream of again.

Maegan Fernandes (13)
Villiers High School, Southall

Victory In The Battlefield

Standing in a battlefield
Watching my fellow mates getting shot down
Terrifying, horrific, deadly, dangerous
However, fighting for my country is more important
In fact, I care more about the country than myself
I care more about my family's safety than mine.

Stepping out of the box of fears is not an easy task
It requires strength and most of all, courage
And the emotion to fight for your country and family.

There I was, watching my best friend getting shot
It was a very painful moment for me
I tried all I could to save her
But she didn't make it
However, I had to move on
She was a brave fighter and died for a good reason
Now it was my turn to avenge her death and fight the opponents.

After hours of shooting
Hours of watching friends die
And hours of watching the opposing army decrease in numbers
It came to a time where they had to surrender
I was proud of myself, the perished and the ones that remained
Those who had passed away got justice

And we proudly fought for our country.

We had won the war
And made our country proud.

Georgina Shinoj (13)
Villiers High School, Southall

Gliding Through Space

Gliding through space
Right after take-off
It makes me feel curious
It makes me feel wonderful!
For am I imagining or is this real?
I am not sure what to believe
That big floating sphere
Or its big floating ring?
What about that shining rock or curious feel
Who knows? None of this might be real
Floating around, thinking of things
I realised what was real
That big floating sphere was a planet
While its ring was more rocks
And that shining thing was a star
I wandered around, taking all this in
For there is much to be done, as well as to discover
I explored the sights, they were more beautiful than the last
This black vacuum we call space
Was more than just empty and vast
It was also a wonder, a carefree feeling
So I wrote down my discoveries on a piece of paper
So when I got back, everyone would know space was more than an endless darkness
Now it will be known as a fascination
A curiosity

I will be a new amazement
Space is more than just a destination beyond Earth
It is a thousand galaxies around us
Or even beyond our universe.

Denisa Chaves (11)
Villiers High School, Southall

I'm No Different From You

They look and they stare
But they never seem to care.
I was brought into this world
Realising life's not fair.

These stereotypes are old
And the world has progressed
So maybe it's time we give it a rest.

All they do is glare
Simply because they can't see my hair.
You do not know me for what's inside,
Just judge the clothing I wear with pride,
I am no different from you!

Just give it a rest,
This is and will always be the way I dress.
Who are you trying to impress?
Because this is my way of being modest.

Hijab is what I choose to wear,
Why do you even care?
I mean it's not rare,
There are people all over the world wearing what I wear.

So be aware,
Don't compare
Because you never know, you might have a pair.

At the end, after all your words,
Criticism and protests
I do not care what others say,
This is who I want to be,
My choice of way.

Sumaya Abdirahman (12)
Villiers High School, Southall

The Eyes Of War

Darkness had descended on Earth,
My atrocious, burgeoning nightmare had given birth,
I distanced myself from humanity,
Drawing closer to an unearthly tragedy,
Withdrawing from the blood of peace,
Shedding blood with destiny,
War was a blazing inferno,
War was bloodshed.

A jet of blood surged into the air,
Wind screamed and slashed my face,
The starless sky was pitch-black and brooding,
As a blood-curdling howl had echoed,
The war had a split second of silence,
Armour was jingling and tinkling under the turbulent cellar-black sky,
A storm of arrows was buzzing through the sky,
Waiting for me to die.

Feet thundered on the valley's cold floor as they bellowed upon us,
I captured the scent of death as I drew closer,
Not long before the raven cawed again,
Where I couldn't hear,
Taking over my footsteps,
Taking me out of existence,

Turning my past into dust,
War was carnage, nothing but carnage.

Rayan Bhuiyan
Villiers High School, Southall

Scared Fish

The life of a fish is hard
When you're being chased by large animals
When a hungry, huge beast swims after you
There is no way of escaping.

The life of a fish is dangerous
As you explore the ocean depths
As soon as we sense danger
We herd into a school of fish.

The life of a fish is miserable
Being eaten at any time
If only we had our own water
With other types of fish.

The life of a fish is sometimes fun
As we explore different areas
We swim in groups
Not knowing the surroundings.

The life of a fish is sometimes fun
As we explore different areas
We swim in groups
Not knowing the surroundings.

The life of a fish is mysterious
Without knowing our future
We don't know when we're going to die
And not knowing what to do in the meantime.

The life of a fish is terrible
Being eaten by predators
No matter what we do
We cannot protect ourselves.

Rayhan Pathak (12)
Villiers High School, Southall

I Am The Knife

I am the killer who haunts your dreams,
The cause of the youths' screams,
Intentions have changed,
Since back in the day,
Nowadays no one plays games,
Knife crime in London,
These kids should be ashamed.

Yes, I am the knife,
I'm the centre of attention on the news nowadays,
"Rising knife crime in London,"
Is all these publishers say.

I am the knife that should lay in your kitchen drawer
But people use me to break the law.
Laws need to be changed,
Streets need to be safe.
We need to tackle this now,
Before there isn't a way.

Guess I should get used to this London life,
From a kitchen, to a pocket, to taking a life,
Is this the life of a knife?
We need to stand up to this, it's real-life.

This is getting out of control,
Innocents dying, losing souls,
Mothers crying,

Children dying,
This isn't how the world should be!

Maaria Mohamed (14)
Villiers High School, Southall

Knife Crime

Crime, crime, crime,
It all comes from crime.
Children are dying,
Dead bodies are lying.
Parents are crying.
Fights happening with knives,
Everybody talks about knife crime.
Schools are dying
When children don't attend.
Youths started smoking,
Nobody is trying to stop it.
Everybody is scared,
Threatened about knives.
Let me ask you a question,
How would you feel if your child had died?
Every kid running from the police,
When the clouds are crying.
Running, cheffing, murders.
His friends gave me a new friend
And his name was Drugs.
He used to keep me tight,
Always used to be by my side,
But now I've stopped,
I'm telling you this 'cause I'm in jail for knife crime.
There is no value in taking a life.
All that's in my head is a new life and a wife.

It all started with a guy with a knife approaching me,
But I didn't know if it was right.

Sukhraj Singh Nagra (13)
Villiers High School, Southall

If Only...

Through the eyes of an autistic child

If only I could speak
I could tell you how I feel
How I feel excited when I see
My favourite song on TV
How I jump, spin and giggle
To show what excites me!

If only I could speak
I could tell you how I feel
How I feel when things aren't how they're supposed to be
When I go into my classroom and everything's changed
How I walk on my toes and scream, running up and down
To show it unsettles me!

If only I could speak
I could tell you how I feel
How I want to say 'I love you Mum and Dad!'
'Cause you never give up on me
How I want to say 'thank you'
For letting me be me!

If only I could speak
I could tell you how I feel
I could tell the world
Don't be blinded by my oddness
How I want you to see
That I have lots of gifts

To share with you and me!
If only I could speak
I could tell you how I feel.

Jasmine Robinson (13)
Villiers High School, Southall

My Deadly Neighbourhood

I take one single step outside the door,
a chill runs down my spine,
my conscience tells me to step back,
my heart tells me to go forward.

It's an ice-cold winter morning,
everything is pitch-black,
I hear voices with every breath I take,
I quietly keep walking.

There are rumours about knife crime,
I'm too petrified to leave my house,
there are over ten crimes committed per week,
my neighbourhood is called The Deadly Neighbourhood.

I can never sleep peacefully at night,
but somehow, I always find a way,
the sun is never out,
the wind growls with pain.

I take one single step outside the door,
everything is pitch-black,
figures/criminals hiding in the shadows,
police say, they're nowhere to be seen.

My heart is pounding with fear,
the rumours take over my inner self,
before I knew it, I was surrounded with darkness...

Diya Jhamat (13)
Villiers High School, Southall

Light To The Darkness

I loved the optimism when I was young
The unknown future made life a daydream.

No one told me the truth
The pain, the anger, the hatred that is shared
By a look, by a word
What have people really come to be?
For racism is around me everywhere
But why does society have to be like this?
You walk down a pathway
Treated differently for the colour of your skin
Your personal beliefs
Your bank status
Hoping that people are better than what they are perceived to be.

I try to believe that people change
But you can't become a better person
When you treat people like they are
On the bottom of your shoe.

I've never heard of justice or freedom, you?
It's a blurry dream that will never be made out
There is hope, right?
But why can't we look for expectations?
Instead of pretending to be okay with reality
Is there a light behind the darkness?

Maleia Dayo Olateju (13)
Villiers High School, Southall

Depression

I could feel the invisible tears running down my face,
Time going slowly, working against me,
The world around me has changed,
Yet I'm still the same.

Wherever I go my mind is still locked up in my room,
Dead inside yet I still live,
I guess God has already decided my doom,
I am my only opponent, it's hard to forgive.

Sadness found me during my happy days,
"Why me?" I ask, it's hard to say,
Will this ever end? The sorrow and the pain,
It's just too hard to amend, I'm living in vain.

I'm drowning in my own tears,
Closing my ears
From the cruel world,
My mind is curled,
I'm dying yet I'm breathing,
Where is this leading?

I will overcome this,
I shall walk through the mist,
I will stand back up again,
I will catch the bullet
And what is depression?
That's the end of the therapy session.

Nithush Gunarajah (13)
Villiers High School, Southall

The Soldier's Goodbye

It is quiet in the bunker, the soldiers are silent
Why do the Nazis have to be violent?
How can we live with the fear of being killed at any moment
Why are the Nazis our opponents?

Alas, it is morning, no time to waste
Time to turn the Nazis into paste
Peering over the bunker, aiming at their heads
Wondering why we want them dead.

I would never understand for I am young
But there are many young people I am among
A Nazi soldier aiming at me
Suddenly, I cannot see.

It is dark, my head is spinning
Distorted faces everywhere, grinning
A light coming closer
Slower and slower.

A beautiful place covered in white
Making the whole room so bright
A voice whispering in my ear
A voice so loud and clear.

He tells me how I die,
How people around me cry and cry
He tells me how he takes the best
And with teary eyes, I begin to rest.

Haaniah Zymal Cadar (11)
Villiers High School, Southall

Taste Of Sri Lanka

I see the world in Sri Lanka.
My eyes glimmer and glisten.
Sri Lanka is glorious, astonishing
and has an alluring scenery.
The sunlight shines on me
and its laugh widens like a hole.
As I walk on the soft sand,
I feel tranquil.
When cars drive, I can hear the radio -
which makes my heart beat like a clock ticking.

There are main foods, rice and curry which
makes my mouth watery and too spicy as a pepper.

The Tamil Tigers,
the liberation who tried to save our Tamil people
live and fight fiercely for our country.
Tamil - one of Sri Lanka's languages
Is what we always respect and love.

The temples we pray in there.
The colourful, bright and beautiful sarees
and glorious jewellery is what we wear.
Sri Lanka is an ecstatic, jubilant country.
Our families and friends
are excited, surprised and astonished to see us in Sri Lanka.

Mathumigaa Kugatheesan (13)
Villiers High School, Southall

Family

A family is a place where you know you can go to,
A family is a place where you can do what you want to do,
A family is a place where people care for you,
A family is a place where you know people will protect you,
Your family will always be there for you.

A family will not let their members down,
A family will let you live with a crown,
A family will see you like you are the night-time sea,
Your family will always be the gold and silver for you and me.

Your family will strengthen you and make you strong,
Your family will correct you when you are wrong,
Your family will give you everything you want,
Your family will stay with you even when they can't.

Your family is a place where dreams come true,
Your family will always want the good for you,
Your family will always support you everywhere you go,
So listen to your family and never say no.

Mischa Fernandes (11)
Villiers High School, Southall

Racism And Me

I have been faced with racism many times
Many times I have had to run away
From the horrors of verbal abuse.

I am courageous and audacious yet disbelieving
Disbelieving of how cruel society can be.

I feel tense and edgy when I walk out into the street
People staring and whispering and pointing at me.

I feel self-conscious and apprehensive when I am in public
I look in every direction and all I see are people pointing and whispering.

Sometimes they come up to me and say words that hurt
I feel like digging up a hole and living in the dirt.

But now I have learnt to stand up
Stand up for what's right.

People no more whisper when I walk past them
They shake hands and ask me to be friends.

My words to all of you are to stand up for yourself
And stand up for what's right.

Japji Kaur Sahota (11)
Villiers High School, Southall

The Ocean

Humans, o' humans,
I cover half of the world
and am the home to most sea creatures,
I am big,
I am blue,
but let me tell something to you,
Humans, o' humans,
look at what you have done to me,
I went from blue to black,
I am a part of the world,
you have stuffed me with plastic
and lost all your love on me,
I am confused,
come help me!
I create enormous waves to the soothing remedy of the wind
and I go up and down to the singing of the whales under me,
but now I don't hear the whales and their music,
that is because of you!
You want to destroy the creatures
and you want to destroy me,
you are creating pollution around the world,
the world is now falling apart,
so are you!

Please save me
and the creatures who live in me.
Please recycle
and make the world good again!

Rishiban Rahuban (11)
Villiers High School, Southall

Tears Of The Earth

You are killing me
I don't want to die
Why don't you see this?
Why, oh why?

I used to be beautiful
My greenery and more
But now I'm too full
Litter reaching the shore.

I'm losing my family
My life, my friends
If you want to live happily
Time to make amends.

You're making me dirty,
You're being so mean
My smell is now nasty
I want to be clean.

There is so much pollution
And stink in the air
There is a solution
Will anyone care?

If my true beauty
Is to be seen
Follow this trinity
To keep me clean.

The first step is reduce
This saves resources
We should also reuse
Let's join forces.

We'll need to recycle
To start our revival
Must stop the denial
For both of our survival.

Zainab Shah (12)
Villiers High School, Southall

Dog's Life

Human! Human!
Wake up! Wake up!
Let's go outside
Let's go!
If you don't wake up, I will lick you
Wake up!
Now!

Human, you don't need shoes
Let's go!
Ah! Fresh air
There is a human there
There is a human there
There is another human
And another!
There are humans everywhere!

Human
Look over there
There is a person who looks like me!
Can I play with him?
Can I?
Why did my friend leave, human?

I need to poo
I need to poo now
I see a tree
Can I poo there?

I am hungry!
Hungry!
I need food now!
Let's go home
And get food!
Ahh! Home sweet home
And food!
Yay!

Why is the sky black, human?
I feel sleepy!
I want to sleep!
Sleep!
Today was a good day...

Swechha Dahal (11)
Villiers High School, Southall

Living On The Streets

Please give me money
Oh, it's no use, they would just ignore as usual
I can't bear panhandling
No warmth, no food, no money.

Same scruffy and smelly clothes
People holding their noses and rushing by
It's been years and years since I left that awful life
All I got is this bag, tattered and so frayed
One pair of socks to call my own
No place for my head to lay.

Late at night in the cold winter
I walk and run
Not too numb to feel
Not too blind to see
My dream long-gone now
Only cold to crystallise my fate.

Can't go anywhere, they say I stink
No food, no water, nowhere to go
Walking out of that home and running until I couldn't run anymore
As you sleep in your warm bed
You should be ashamed walking with your heads high
And your noses pinched.

Kamaldeep Rehal (13)
Villiers High School, Southall

The Life Of The Endangered

I've been all alone,
It was just myself,
It was just me in the cruel world,
After my precious home was destroyed
By those selfish humans.

Their use of these so-called 'cars',
The mechanical beasts destroyed my home,
Releasing filth in the air,
Making the world warmer,
Destroying my icy home.

I now wander the white, snowy plains,
Barely getting enough food,
Hunting on my own is hard,
I'm coming closer to death with every day that goes by,
I don't know how much longer I can go on like this.

I now lie here,
The icy snow slowly creeping over me,
As I take my final breaths,
The ice breaks around me
And I start to helplessly sink into the freezing water,
The final image I see is a snowy plain
And the destruction of humanity.

Yaqub Bodak Jaan (12)
Villiers High School, Southall

I Know God Is With Me

Of all the paths I cross, I know God is with me
When I held the stoner's coats, I know God was with me
Of when I breathed murderous threats against the Lord's disciples, I know his eyes were on me
When I turned blind, I know the Lord spoke to me
When Ananias placed his hands on me, I know God was with me
When I got baptised, I know the Lord Almighty rejoiced over me
When I started preaching that Jesus was our saviour, I know the Lord spoke through me
When others heard me and believed, I know God was performing miracles using me
When people planned to kill me, I know God was beside me
When Silas and I were put into prison, I know the Father who art in Heaven rescued me
When I travelled to synagogues, temples and churches
I know God looked after me
Of all the paths I cross, I know God is with me.

Epziba Paramasivam (12)
Villiers High School, Southall

Mother Nature's Woes

Once upon a time
Children played together,
From hopscotch to marbles and rock-paper-scissors.
The childhood from the past was filled with gladness and joy,
But that is not true in this era, my dear boy.

How advanced are the children of the future?
Like small adults with tiny, interesting frames
They grow up so fast in the speed-operated culture.

But where are the morning birds and the green trees
For them to play with?
The creeping grass and the busy bees?

I like to see a pink flower, but I hate to see a plucked flower,
I like to be in the chilly breeze,
But I don't like to be in the filthy grease.
I like to see plants increase
But I hate to see plants decrease.

To plant a tree we take more time
But to destroy a tree we take less time, why?

Cavan Goes (13)
Villiers High School, Southall

You Did This!

Why did you do this?
What did I do to deserve this?
I am sadly dying
While your economies are flying.
Stop this destruction,
This is corruption.

You and your economies
Think about our environment,
This is very tragic
But something can fix it,
It is the magic of awareness.

I am the cause of your lives,
I can help and provide
But you care only about money
And you think it is funny!
I provide things like food, water and shelter,
But it's not enough, not enough for you.

I am breaking apart,
You broke my heart,
It's time to start,
Start to realise and help,
That I am your saviour.

You are blinded by money,
You don't care about me,

To solve this big equation
You must help me as I am the Earth.

Kirath Pal (12)
Villiers High School, Southall

My Dear Daughter

My daughter is very curious, very.
She never leaves my side,
It's like we're stuck with super glue.
Argh!
The thing that she has done all of her life,
Is hold my hand.
I'm thinking, *how will she hold my hand when she's married?*
Sukhmani is very independent,
Just like a lion,
And is just as fierce as a tiger,
But on the outside,
She's graceful as a swan,
She knows she is.

I love her dearly,
Especially when she cuddles me in her arms.
Me in her arms,
Her skin is so soft, just like a newborn baby's skin.
Her cheeks glow red,
When she's happy,
And her happy face turns into a frown when she's unhappy,
But I always love her dearly,
When she's happy or sad.

My loving daughter,
Sukhmani.

Sukhmani Bhachu (11)
Villiers High School, Southall

The Imaginary City

One day I woke up early in the morning...
Dreaming about an imaginary city.
It would be as big as half a continent
And as wide as Europe.

There would be skyscrapers in every single part,
The houses would be as luxurious as a hotel
And there would be no problem with the food,
The city's five-star chefs would cook delicious meals all day long.

Every morning you'd wake up and meet kind people,
They'd help you, cheer you up and even talk with you.
If you're low on income, don't worry,
This city has an excellent amount of jobs to choose from.

Who knows, this imaginary city could be real
Or it could just be a dream in the past.
I'm hoping my imaginary city is real
And I'll keep on wishing till the last day of my life...

Hatim (12)
Villiers High School, Southall

Why Me?

Why me?
Out of everybody you see.
What do I lack?
Am I a maniac?
Is it the flawless skin
Or is my existence a deadly sin?

I ask of you one thing,
To stop pinching
Like a bee sting.
I hide away every day,
Hoping I'm not someone's prey.
Will today be the day?

You did a great job with those words,
They really hit me hard, like swords.
Every daring day I was abused
And went back home bruised.
My heart was broken into pieces
And within the cracks grew depression and diseases.

This very heart wasn't about to repair so easily,
As it had been hurt grievously.
One day I just gave up
Because life had screwed up.
I was over with this crazy adventure
And that was the end of my successful future.

Munazza Khalid (13)
Villiers High School, Southall

Love, Die And Reunite

My eyes were opened during my search
Two birds found in the middle of the green nature
I was being separated far and far
Some of me dark and some of me light.

Mother Nature had bowed down at them
Looking at a one and only unbelievable sight
Where a man and woman reunite
Love had shown its presence on Earth.

Alone. Alone. Left them both alone
Dark had taken over bright
Mother Nature was sad
Darkness and sadness evolved.

Looked around the dark, empty field
Sadness took the countryside
How lonely it felt
Gave the sense of bad times.

Went around the globe
Came back to the same place
The same woman dressed in white
Sobbing at her dead husband's body
And this was the end of their life.

Himesh Vijai Valgi (12)
Villiers High School, Southall

Death Row

The jail bars rattle 25th June
The end is near, the end is soon
I rise still tired to see a midnight moon
I sleep again, knowing the end is soon.

"Wake up!" the guard shouts as I wake from my dream
I wake up to reality, upset things aren't as they seem
I look around, look around at my room
The end is near, the end is soon.

I finish my last meal, the empty plate is red
"It's time to go, it's time to leave," he said
I walk slowly with my head up to the room
The end is near, the end is soon.

As I sit on my chair I have a thought of death row
I feel scared... expressionless thoughts
I feel something on my cheek, the smallest, tiniest tear
The end has come, the end is here.

Yash Sangani (13)
Villiers High School, Southall

Toddler Life

Life as a toddler is fun
Many people surrounding me
I joke around and make puns
But my life is not interesting without pretend tea.

Many kisses and hugs
Even though I'm cheeky
The only thing that scares me is bugs
When no parents are looking, I turn sneaky.

Watching Peppa Pig is life
But I still have to go to nursery
When I go there, people take care of me which makes me feel safe
Though it is still a misery.

Now my mum is pregnant
I am going to be a big sister
This makes me so excited that my mum is pregnant
I can't wait to find out if the baby is my brother or sister.

This is the end
Hopefully I can write another poem after the baby is out.

Deepshika Kamalakasan (11)
Villiers High School, Southall

Hope

I wake up every day,
only to be in more pain.
I hide in the corner and cry away
and hope for them to use their brain.
To stop harming wildlife
and cutting down trees.
Yet still they stab with a knife
and put oil in my seas.
Every day I hope.

I wake up every day
and see garbage everywhere.
I wish and pray
that they would care.
I choke and cough
because pollution has spread all over.
I need to stay tough
but I roll over.
Every day I hope.

I wake up every day
with terrible headaches.
I am starting to decay
with no water in my lakes.
Please help me, someone
to save these creatures.
To destroy that gun

and become a teacher.
Every day I hope.

Mian Waleed Ahmad (13)
Villiers High School, Southall

The Cat

The cat that was fat,
liked eating and chasing rats,
although life was a mystery.
It had a lot of knowledge of history,
it sat on a mat,
waiting for the rat,
to become its dinner.
Although the rat was thinner,
the cat was a beginner.

The cat had a dream,
it was as weird as it seems.
It wanted to see England,
and have freshly baked beans.

Vroom!
There was a beam!
Everything went dark,
no sound,
not even a London dog barked!
Everything was quiet,
it was weird,
the cat felt as if it had a beard.
Wait, what?
The cat was flying!
He looked down and saw the rat!

It said, "Haha, you're dying!"
The cat's last moments...

Kahin Alemayehu (11)
Villiers High School, Southall

The End

I couldn't believe my eyes
There everyone was
They were lying on the ground
With blood spreading from their bullet-impaled bodies
Corpses everywhere
Families mourning their lost ones everywhere
I wished I was blind.

I couldn't believe my ears
Screams everywhere
Gunshots killing everyone
I could hear the cries of the dying soldiers
It almost brought me to tears
I wished I was deaf.

I couldn't believe my nose
The stench of drying blood
The stench of rotten corpses
The smell of gunpowder in the air
I wished I was nose-blind.

I had enough
I couldn't handle it
Everybody else was dead
So I decided to join them.

Aditya Bhandari (12)
Villiers High School, Southall

The Old Man

I saw a gloomy old man
Whose smile only weighed a gram
I said, "If you tell me what's wrong, I'll do what I can!"
He just sat there as cold as a clam.

He did not move, not once!
Never did decide to look
Just smoked out of his pipe
Reading his dusty old book.

He kept getting older and older
He now had long hair and a beard
The room felt colder, way colder
He finally looked up as he sneered
His image got lighter and lighter
As his hair got whiter and brighter.

This sad man drew nearer and nearer
As I felt closer to him, much dearer
The truth became clearer, way clearer
That this old man was me - staring into a mirror.

Abdirahman Awmusse (11)
Villiers High School, Southall

My Life

I was born in 1902
And my name is Andrew.
This is a story about me
That I recommend you read.

I lost my parents at a young age,
It put my life inside a cage.
Now it was just me and my brother
And we did not get along.

I was thirty when I had my first child
And so, I named him Kyle,
But suddenly he died
And my wife and I just cried.

We thought it was over
Just like the life of a clover.
But then I had a glimmer of hope,
That said I have to cope.

So you need to live life at the fullest of dreams
Which may be harder than it seems.
But if you can put your heart into it,
Then hard tasks will become as small as a nit.

Zakaria Abdelrahman (12)
Villiers High School, Southall

Optimism
Through the eyes of an immigrant

Rushing through the green, thorny leaves
Petrified, impetuously crawling,
Hoping my knees don't snap
Frantically I remember my fundamental dream.

Trees dancing around,
Symbolising the catastrophic truth
I am a migrant, scurrying for food
And a better life
I am not prestigious,
This is persuading me to enter America.

In the distance, my sight catches some security
Wearing green and white
Guards as gigantic as Hulk
And as sad as an upside down rainbow.

Provoking awareness, no one less significant in the world
It is the same as how God made the world
Just be optimistic
You will achieve anything.

Priyesh Kanji (13)
Villiers High School, Southall

Animals' Home

Roses are red
Violets are blue
Stop cutting the trees
The animals die too.

They lose their habitat
They have to run
Why are you a scaredy-cat?
They lost their mums.

Why are you cutting the trees?
That's a mistake
You don't pay fees
Your lies are a mistake.

Animals go extinct
It's your fault
You need to rethink
You're gonna haunt.

It's your fault the animals die
So help them
Stop cutting them
And end your mistake.

Imagine all the oxygen we lose
It's your fault
So help the environment
And stop cutting the trees

#TeamTrees
Please donate.

Kamaljeet Kukrija (12)
Villiers High School, Southall

How Would You Feel?

How would you feel
If you couldn't see blue?
The colour of the tranquil, alleviating ocean,
The colour of the high and mighty sky,
The colour of heavenly happiness.

How would you feel
If you couldn't see red?
The colour of healthy blood,
The colour of healthy strawberries,
The colour of luxurious love.

How would you feel
If you couldn't see green?
The colour of dewy fields in spring,
The colour of fiery chilli,
The colour of emulous envy.

How would you feel
If you couldn't see colour at all?
Your eyes deceiving you
With every passing second,
That's how I feel.

Yuvika Tulcidas (12)
Villiers High School, Southall

The Last Moment

I hadn't been feeling happy in years,
I sat there in the sea of memories,
Overflowing me,
Drowning in the sea of memories,
Mourning the death of me.

The doctor rushed outside,
Hearing shouting and screaming,
The door flapped open,
Came in my daughter, squeaking.

My eyes overflowed with tears,
As I said my last words,
As my daughter heard,
She couldn't stop weeping.

As I was speaking,
I just remembered,
Her brother now wailing,
Now I remembered.

"Look after him," I muttered,
Hoping she would understand,
I repeated,
"Look after..."

Muhammed Hassan Abdulmanem (11)
Villiers High School, Southall

Who Am I?

Who am I?
I look into the children's eyes
And they feel a wave of warmth rush over them
I care, love and help
Just to fulfil their dreams.

Who am I?
Do you know?
I speed to their danger
Like a cheetah saving its cub
The children can't fool me
I know when they're lying!

Who am I?
I hate when someone tells them off
I hate when they're upset
When I see the children only
I wish, I wish it were me who was hurt.

Who am I?
I am a mother
I am the guardian of my children
No one understands this job
No pay or rest
However, I get the best payment
Love.

Harshpreet Kaur (11)
Villiers High School, Southall

Life Of An Orphan

Mummy,
Daddy,
Where did you go?
I need you because I feel so much sorrow.

I feel so alone
but I don't want to moan
because you might come home,
but that might not be true
as the evil man buried you.

Everyone is happy yet I am sad
why do they all treat me this bad?
I don't go to school,
I have no friends
but they pick on me because they're cool
and this might be my end.

I am so hungry,
I feel so much despair,
I want someone to hug me
but they won't dare.

So Mummy, Daddy
please look over me
and make me feel some glee,
not angry.

Ridwanul Yamim (12)
Villiers High School, Southall

Isolation

My identity is like a box
Trapped sadly with no freedom
I sit lonely in class
Doing nothing
Everyone asks, I shake my head
With nothing to say.

My brain tells me nothing
But it might tell me something
Go and search for it.

I got up, go around and around
Everywhere
Trying to search for my key to life.

Autumn, winter, summer runs past
And still, no identity for me.

Mum hasn't bought cherries
But bought berries
Also a parcel, a curious, keen desperate one
It is for me
I open it but sadly
Sadly it is empty
My identity is... nothing.

Anoshan Selvanathan (14)
Villiers High School, Southall

Friends, Friends

Friends, friends
What do they do?
They always take care of you.

Friends, friends
Honest and kind
But somehow, they are always hard to find.

Friends, friends
They are always there for you
When we're together, we shout, "Woohoo!"

Friends, friends
Whenever you're sad
They'll be there and they'll be glad.

Friends, friends
No matter what comes
They will be there for you to make you shine.

Friends, friends
Short hair and chubby cheeks
They are different to you
But that's what makes them unique.

Navdeep Kaur (11)
Villiers High School, Southall

He Doesn't Stop

He grabs her by the neck.
She struggles to even breathe.
Her life starts to bend
As she goes down on her knees.

He pulls her hair back.
Her luscious blonde curls.
He ties her hands,
The pain starting to burn.

She screams for help
As he says he loves her.
He doesn't stop,
Her blood floats on murky water.

She struggles to resist.
The fire burning her skin.
She has nothing left to lose.
She has nothing left to give.

Suddenly, the pain starts to fade
As she sees a bright light.
He finally stops
As she closes her eyes.

Mustafa Suleman (13)
Villiers High School, Southall

A Harsh Perspective

My brain talks in maths and buzzes like a fridge
Some say my eyes are lifeless
Flightless like a deformed bird
I try to move forward.

My words are like an untuned radio
Fuzzy behind the madness
Every day it gets harder to think
I try to move forward.

The illness in my mind shackles me to the ground
Colours are fading, fading from the falling sky
An everlasting funeral surrounds my soul
I try to move forward.

I can no longer try to be a walking starlight
A moment I'll never remember and a fight I'll never forget
I stop moving forward.

Safa Noor Aurangzaib (13)
Villiers High School, Southall

A Wise Man

A wise man once said...
A man's life is what his thoughts make,
Plant a seed in your brain,
Water it, nurture it
Until you bloom.

A wise man once said...
A man is what he thinks about all day,
Even though you've bloomed
You need more water and nurturing
Or you'll gradually descend, head in arms back to your grave.

A wise man once said...
Human beings can alter their lives by altering their attitudes of mind.
Two seeds, one corn, one poison,
Land will give you just what you wanted,
An abundance of corn and poison just like our brains.

Agreem Pradhan (13)
Villiers High School, Southall

PS4 Life

I can't wait,
I can't wait,
It's almost Friday,
Meaning I can play!

Yes, it's Friday,
Now all I need to do is wait.
He's up and ready,
So let's play!

PS4 on,
Now what shall we play?
Fortnite, Injustice or Spider-Man, hey!
Fortnite it is, okay.

What skin should we put?
What mode should we do?
Fun, fun, fun, that's what we do,
My player is best.

No, no, no, no,
Iqbal has to sleep,
I have to wait 'til tomorrow,
But I can't, I'm too impatient!
See ya later, Iqbal G.

Iqbal Garewal (11)
Villiers High School, Southall

But, Who Am I?

I love you without knowing you
I have to abandon you
Tell me what to do
Some people judge me
Some people hate me
But, who am I?

In fact, hate me
Love me
I don't care
War, after war
Death, after death
But, who am I?

This country is my mother
And now
I have to live without her
But, who am I?

People judge me
Politics fighting
What is the point
Of a war?
But, who am I?

Animals dying
But not just
For global warming

Also for war
Of hate and love
But, who am I?

Ines Ranzan Shil (12)
Villiers High School, Southall

The Decision

Just a woman
In a dark and dull world,
No one knows what I am thinking
And no one will want to know.

Every day I see women fighting for their rights,
But all women were ignored
And also not respected
And there came my job.

I will fight for our rights until we get what we want,
When equality takes over the world,
That is when everything will change
And when we will live with pride.

This will be the moment when we can have our say,
When we can make decisions
And when we can be equal and fair
And live happily forever.

Johan Virgil Mariyathas (12)
Villiers High School, Southall

The Boy Who Was Always Sad

The rain poured,
His heart poured with sadness.
The cloud growled at him,
He was abandoned.
His heart was as dark as a black stone,
His life was murky and dim.

He gazed at the dull, shadowed sky.
Crash!
He sought for shelter,
He knew a storm was coming.

Deserted and isolated,
The young boy hid under the table.

The rain poured,
His heart pounded,
He saw an immense shadow.

Depressed and sorrowful,
The boy sat in pity.

He was abandoned,
His tears were a never-ending fountain.

Hibo Omar Abdallah (11)
Villiers High School, Southall

Extinction

Humans
When will they ever learn?
Instead of building things
Why don't they plant trees?
Do they want to suffocate?

Instead of fighting
Why don't they talk it out?
It's common knowledge
That violence isn't the key
Or is it not so common anymore?

I hope the humans
Know they're just causing
Their own extinction.

I would do something
Anything
But what can a
Mere unintelligent birdy
Like myself do?

Better nothing
Than something
Stupid like
The humans.

Musabeha Tuqeer Cheema (14)
Villiers High School, Southall

Frightening Things

I wanted to go on a walk,
I didn't want to talk,
I hope you understand why,
It's just a teenage thing,
Trust me, it will go by,
Then I see a ring.

I walk up by it,
I see a flash,
Next to it, I see a kit,
As I get closer, I get a rash,
I think it was the poison ivy,
But then I see my friend, Ivy.

I don't get scared easily,
I ain't silly,
I turn back and go home,
I thought I was alone,
I then see Ivy,
My rash turned green like 'ivy'.

I woke up, it was all a dream.

Ashwinder Kaur (12)
Villiers High School, Southall

My Body

I think my owner loathes me.
He shoves sweets into me,
He smokes 24/7,
He eats enough to feed an elephant.
When will he ever stop?

Last night, he was sleeping
And sleeping
And sleeping.
Another inhale of toxin.
He never exhales,
He is bigger than a hippo.
Because of him,
All I have in me is fat,
Fat!

I hate him!
I hate him for what he has done to me!
When will he ever stop?
The night before that,
He was smoking.
My last inhale of toxin
And how did I end up?
Dead!

Amadou Bente Diallo (12)
Villiers High School, Southall

Heartbroken

Heart-warming smiles
Joyful laughter
How I wish they were real
How do they feel?
I feel like a servant.
Have I always been a left-out kid?
They say, "Tell a teacher how you feel."
If I had real parents, they would listen to me.
Just alone, always, always.
How do I feel?
Like a coward, like a rat.
Is this the life of a boy who has cancer?
Is this the life of an orphan?
Is this normal?
I am a dreadful burden, aren't I?
I wish I died.
Is this normal?
Are hearts meant to be broken?

Jagman Singh (11)
Villiers High School, Southall

My Sister, The Tyrant

Woken in the morning with a fist in my head
Fist in my head, fist in my head
"Go fetch my shoes, they're under your bed
Under your bed, under your bed."
I have a bump on my head, I soon may be dead
Soon may be dead, soon may be dead
I hate her so much, I will go in the shed
Go hide in the shed, go hide in the shed
Now that I'm done, let's go have some fun
Let's go have some fun, let's go have some fun
Oh no! She wants to have fun, but I just wanna run
I just wanna run, I just wanna run.

Shreya Jadeja (11)
Villiers High School, Southall

The End

I can see from your eyes
The end of the world.

I can see people
Running around for help.

I can see that the sky is red
Like fire will come out of it.

I can see many aeroplanes
In the sky that is red.

I can see people running over each other
And children crying.

I can see why this is happening
Because we are using so much plastic.

I can see that we are using many things
That affect the Earth in a bad way.

At last, I can see
That everything is destroyed.

Oshita Katial (12)
Villiers High School, Southall

To Look Normal

I wonder how it feels to look normal,
I ponder every day.
Maybe tomorrow, I'll wake up and look okay,
Or maybe I won't and I'll ponder the next day.

Henry's my name,
But most people call me lame,
I feel alone,
As the darkness fills the room.

It's my dream to look different,
I feel left out,
I'll always hope,
'Til my last day on this Earth.

Why me?
Why can't people understand?
Why do I look this way?
I need answers,
Now!

Najma Muhyidin Bundid (11)
Villiers High School, Southall

Ronaldo

I am your inspiration
I am the light of football
I am strong
I am famous
I am rich
I am out of this world.

I skill players with ease
I nutmeg them
I roulette them
I rainbow flick them
I dribble past them.

I score amazing goals
Bottom left corner
Bottom right corner
Top right corner
Top left corner
Post and in
Crossbar and in.

I help the poor
I sold the Golden Boot
And gave the money to the poor
And I am really cool.

Arashnoor Singh (11)
Villiers High School, Southall

Too Late

Screaming! Shots in the air,
It was like no one even cared.
Mum was there on the floor,
I had to run to the shore.
Black bag on my head,
For weeks, I wasn't fed.
Then I heard a boom!
Someone was in my room.
They said it was my time,
As it was nine.
Bang!
I saw fire,
I heard bells,
I was in Hell.
I prayed the pain wouldn't last,
If only they knew my past.
They identified me as Jack from Camberley,
Who would give the bad news to my family?

Jayden Masih (11)
Villiers High School, Southall

Miss Cosmas

I am Miss Cosmas
The graceful librarian
My job is to help children
Succeed and get better.

My library is a beach of serenity
Where children can enjoy reading books
This is how my fellow companions work.

However, I do not tolerate bad behaviour
My library will never have trouble
So please do not misbehave with me
Dealing with children is a cup of tea.

I am Miss Cosmas
The graceful librarian
I love my job so much
It is irreplaceable.

Jamal Aidan Khan (11)
Villiers High School, Southall

School And Best Friends

Here, we are best friends.
Your name is Hikari.
My name is Maham.
We are best friends.

We were new in the school.
We were confused in the school.
The school is really cool.
We were really new in the school.

Me and Hikari were happy.
We were excited to see.
Me and Hikari were confused.
Me and Hikari were happy.

We are best friends forever.
We are friends.
We have never been angry to each other.
We are best friends forever.

Maham Fatima Ashraf Begum (11)
Villiers High School, Southall

It's Just Too Deep

I try to force myself to sleep
But all I feel are my tears as they seep;
The mark on the arm and the scar on the cheek
Are just too deep.

The idea of evil oppressors
I don't want to keep;
The fear of the tormentors
Is just too deep.

The pressure of going to school
Just makes me weep;
The message from my heart
Is just too deep.

This pain, this distress,
No one will peep;
This feeling, this loneliness
Is just too deep.

Bedanta Mukhopadhay (12)
Villiers High School, Southall

Where Did The Snow Go?

Where did the snow go?
Away it went with one big blow.
No,
Then what happened to the lustrous glow
Of the beautiful sheet of pale white snow?
It melted,
I know,
So sorrow,
Because all of these careless humans' heads are hollow,
All of these fossil fuels,
They create harm to our beautiful and brilliant zone of 'o',
But anyway,
Goodbye, farewell,
For I am melting now,
Oh no.
Oh, humans please tell us,
Where did the snow go?

Nadal Makoto Spencer-Jennings (12)
Villiers High School, Southall

Mum

She constantly works every day
She thinks we are not working
She is like a star
She may not realise that she works hard all day
Maybe she also forgets to take care of herself
She shines at night
She makes everything go right
Whenever she is here
Nothing wrong can happen
She shines like a moon in the dark night
She is bright as a sun
She knows when I am sad
Or when I'm happy
I love her the most
And I know she loves me as well.

Manal Khan (12)
Villiers High School, Southall

Plastic

Imagine the screaming of animals,
Asking you to save them.
The ozone layer will soon get damaged,
So stop littering.
What you do hurts animals!
You must be the change you wish to see in the world
Or soon our oldest friends will die,
With the hands of the careless, evil god.
Plastic will soon take our friends away,
With one bite, they cannot eat
As we have blocked their throats
And soon will die of starvation all because of us,
Humans!

Diya Patel (12)
Villiers High School, Southall

The Librarian Of Villiers High School

Welcome to our library
Please take a book
And if you don't know what to do
I'll help you with it.

Are you into fantasy or adventure?
Or are you into science fiction?
I'll help you with choosing a book
I'll make sure you'll enjoy it.

If you're upset or sad
I'll always give you a hand
Our library is very friendly
And we will look after you carefully.

Arthy Vasikaran (11)
Villiers High School, Southall

Pollution In The Ocean

I am...
Beautiful, powerful, graceful.
I care about the plants and animals that live in me.
I cover 71% of the Earth
And yet you still don't take care of me.
I care about anti-pollution
But you still litter me.
Every day my strength fades away from me,
Everything is changing in me.
I helped you, so please help me.
The more pollution, the more pain in me.
People must help, please.

Piranusha Mohanathas (12)
Villiers High School, Southall

Primary School

When they say you'll be fine
They forget
About homework
The size
And leaving everyone
So that they leave you
And you leave them
At first you don't believe them
Then slowly, your mind changes
And you start to believe
And get used to it all
You get used to homework
You won't get lost
And all the people you left
Will simply be a memory.

Kelsi Ramsey-Carney (11)
Villiers High School, Southall

The End

I keep wishing and wishing
As my resources are finishing
Trees do so much for all
That every day I see them fall
Pollution spreading everywhere
The land, water and air
Even the sight of a star is rare
Humans are just wrecking me
Plastic flooding every sea
I know they will flee
Leaving the chaos behind
Making it the end of mankind.

Jaslin Malotra (13)
Villiers High School, Southall

Who Am I?

I am from a different country.
People call me dumb, ugly, weak.
People are laughing at me.
People call me unknown,
Hoping I will tell you my feelings but I can't.
People identify my languages, religion.
Where you are born, values
And beliefs you are taught.
Why you look like that?
Why my colour is dark on light?
What is your name?

Ramisa Ali (13)
Villiers High School, Southall

Bullying

Bullying could affect your heart,
Your mentality,
Physically and emotionally.
It makes you go to your room,
Sitting in the corner
Just hating yourself, it's just diminishing.

It takes over you with depression,
That strangles you by the neck
And takes over
And then you ask yourself,
"Is there a purpose in living?"

Kaelem Rai (13)
Villiers High School, Southall

Life Of A Bird

From up above
the world
is small
and everything looks different.
You would not
recognise it at all
from up where
the clouds
are drifting.
All the colours
red, blue and green.
From up
there, it's
a beautiful scene.
A wonderful sight
to see
if you
were
flying with
me.

Anson Fernandes (11)
Villiers High School, Southall

A Rainy Day, A Windy Day, A Sunny Day

I can see the waves dashing
The clouds crying
The wind is blowing
And we are flying.

The rain is pouring
The waters are flowing
The clouds are running
And people are walking.

The clouds are moving
The sun is rising and shining
A rainy day, a windy day
Sunny day, we all are enjoying.

Julinka Pereira (12)
Villiers High School, Southall

Money Has A Life

Money,
It's a beautiful thing,
We go outside and spend it all,
But we don't seem to notice it,
We are wasting trees,
It is an ugly thing,
We go outside and spend it all,
You will notice it when there's no CO_2 left,
Stop wasting trees!

Abdul Asslan (12)
Villiers High School, Southall

The Life Of A Cat

Cute twirly things bouncing up and down
Fluffy as can be
Although they have different personalities you see
One can do backflips
One can eat chips
Out of all pets, cats will soar above
True they may be naughty but they fill your heart with love.

Inaya Ahmed (11)
Villiers High School, Southall

No Love In War

War is heartless
with soldiers that are careless.
They don't care before killing
but always think of surviving.
Everywhere is destruction
kids being sold at auction.
Tanks stamping the roads
like killing people with swords.

Tarnbeer Singh (13)
Villiers High School, Southall

Animals

I saw, I saw, I saw
Animals running
I saw, I saw, I saw
Animals getting hurt.
I saw, I saw, I saw
Animals dying.
I saw...
The humans...

Murthad Abdalla (11)
Villiers High School, Southall

Refugee Child

Your biggest fear right now
Is homework
Mine is being able to survive.

You can walk home safely
Do things you love
I keep running
Where? I don't know
I run, I swim, even crawl to safety
I still haven't found it
I've never felt 'safe'
I've just guessed it's somewhere
Peaceful and happy
But again, what is 'peaceful' and 'happy'?
The only feelings I've experienced
Are fear and hope.

You don't have to run
Leaving your family behind
Swim to another country
Without drowning
Have you watched your family
Die in front of your eyes?
Should a child even go through that?
I do
Every day.

I wish to live life like you
I wish to learn
I wish to sleep
Without terrifying nightmares waking me up
I wish to enjoy time with friends
I wish to laugh so hard my tummy aches
I wish to run in long, green grass
And not on painful, solid rocks
I could achieve this
With your help
Your love, your care
You decide my future.

Beca Fon Parry (13)
Ysgol Brynrefail, Caernarfon

A Life In The Sea

I am a tiny turtle
With no place to go
My home is no longer safe
I'm really sure you know.

You might know about my troubles
My struggles to find safe food
You might know about my sadness
For I'm singing the blues.

No more smiling children
No more happy families
You're killing all of my people
Soon we won't be in the seas.

Plastic is taking over
Invading our beautiful homes
Filling up our feeding grounds
We really need some help!

There are some incredible people
Who help to clean up the seas
But they can't do it alone
Save our families, please!

I am a tiny turtle
With no place to go
My home is no longer safe
And everybody knows.

Libby Cole (13)
Ysgol Clywedog, Wrexham

Cross Me Out

C aring and comforting, I thought you were
R uthless and rude, you turned out to be
O ut and about, you cross me out
S mile at me when people are around
S tole my everything when I was gone.

M ean and manipulative, that's just you
E nvy and enmity run through your veins.

O nly one I had, to share my feelings with
U nder your breath, my name you take
T ables have turned, you have gone down.

Atiya Ahmed (12)
Ysgol Clywedog, Wrexham

Chopping Trees

Chopping trees is no good
We are the lungs of the world
But you are killing off our neighbourhood
The leaves around you will be curled.

Help us, please
I cannot breathe
The air is filled with smoke
They are cutting beneath
And cutting my heart.

Chopping trees is no good
They have to cut me down
So they have no air
Don't save me but save my friends.

Sarah Roberts (13)
Ysgol Clywedog, Wrexham

YOUNG WRITERS INFORMATION

We hope you have enjoyed reading this book – and that you will continue to in the coming years.

If you're a young writer who enjoys reading and creative writing, or the parent of an enthusiastic poet or story writer, do visit our website www.youngwriters.co.uk. Here you will find free competitions, workshops and games, as well as recommended reads, a poetry glossary and our blog. There's lots to keep budding writers motivated to write!

If you would like to order further copies of this book, or any of our other titles, then please give us a call or order via your online account.

Young Writers
Remus House
Coltsfoot Drive
Peterborough
PE2 9BF
(01733) 890066
info@youngwriters.co.uk

Join in the conversation!
Tips, news, giveaways and much more!

YoungWritersUK   @YoungWritersCW